Multiplying Love

Multiplying Love

A Vision of United Methodist Life Together

Paul W. Chilcote

Abingdon Press
Nashville

MULTIPLYING LOVE

ISBN: 978-1-7910-3281-4
Library of Congress Control Number: 2023944591

Scripture quotations unless noted otherwise are from the Common English Bible. Copyright © 2011 by the Common English Bible. All rights reserved. Used by permission. www.CommonEnglishBible.com.

Contents

Acknowledgments 1

Our Purpose 3

Part I. Love and Unity in a Renewed
United Methodist Church

    1. Always Renewing 13

    2. Love Is the Highest Gift 23

    3. Why We Need to Embrace Unity 33

    4. The Peaceable Reign of Christ 41

    Study and Discussion Questions for Part I 51

Part II. A Renewed Wesleyan Movement of
Inclusive Love

    5. The Opportunity Before Us 55

    6. The Church as a Community of Inclusive
Love and Grace. 65

    7. Discovering Love Again for the First Time 75

    8. A Vision for the Refreshed
United Methodist Church. 85

    Study and Discussion Questions for Part II 95

Epilogue. 97

Endnotes 101

Sources 107

Acknowledgments

A "fire in my belly" produced this book. Perhaps it would be better to say a "warmed heart." I completed the manuscript during a period of work and study at two British institutions. My first debt of gratitude, therefore, goes to the staff and students who welcomed me back to Wesley House, Cambridge, and supported me in my time there.

Secondly, every year I lead a group of pilgrims to historic sites related to John and Charles Wesley and the birth of the Methodist movement. Sarum College in Salisbury functions as our base. Staying in the cathedral close is enough to inspire anyone. Thanks to all at Sarum for the hospitality they provided and the space to reflect and write on the periphery of that journey. The juxtaposition of visits to Epworth, Oxford, Bristol, and London—where Methodism was born—deeply informed these reflections on the future of our beloved United Methodist Church. I thank the pilgrims with whom I shared conversations about the future of the church. These dear people give me hope.

Many colleagues and friends reflected with me on the original

1

draft of this book and prayed for its completion. I so deeply appreciate their questions, comments, and insights as well as their personal support and encouragement. Many thanks to Tom Berlin, Allan Bevere, Ashley Boggan, Bob Bushong, David Byrum, Lynn Caldwell, Kenneth H. Carter, Magrey deVega, June Edwards, Heather Harding, Jim Harnish, Steve Harper, Sue Haupert-Johnson, Jean Hawxhurst, Elaine Heath, Christy Holden, James Howell, Karen Oliveto, Jon Priebe, Jen Whitmore, Alice Williams, Jan Yandell, and last but not least, my dear wife of nearly fifty years, Janet, who helped me birth every book I published.

The staff at Abingdon Press have been wonderful. I am particularly grateful to Neil Alexander who saw the value in moving my manuscript quickly into print. The primary editor behind the scenes evaluates, thinks, sorts, rephrases, and polishes a manuscript to turn it into a book, and seldom gets the credit they deserve. Credit here belongs to my good friend, Paul Franklyn. Many thanks to you and those who worked the process, whose names I may never know.

Finally, I want to express my appreciation to all those people in my life who taught me that nothing, nothing is more important than love. Many of them are now "lost in wonder, love, and praise" (Charles Wesley, "Love Divine") and "have the power to grasp love's width and length, height and depth, together with all believers" (Ephesians 3:18-19). I pray we may all be filled, one day, with the fullness of God.

Our Purpose

In September 2022, Jeff Greenway (a former United Methodist pastor from Pennsylvania) and Mike Lowry (a recently retired United Methodist bishop from Texas) published a book entitled *Multiplying Methodism*. Their book is an appeal for congregations to disaffiliate from The United Methodist Church (UMC) to align their congregations and membership with the breakaway Global Methodist Church (GMC).

After publishing more than thirty books, this is my first book to function as a rebuttal to what someone else published. I am compelled, out of love for the church, and with respect for authors I counted as colleagues, to provide a different vision from their "Bold Witness of Wesleyan Faith at the Dawn of the Global Methodist Church."

Like many Methodist people, I try to avoid confrontation. Since Jeff and Mike's book appeared a year earlier than this rebuttal, a response will not likely fall on receptive ears among those who have now left The United Methodist Church. So this response is first an appeal to those who are still in discernment about what to do. "Do we stay or do we go?" God's peace is deserved by those who have left and those who might leave. But for those still in discernment mode, this book offers a vision of a renewed United Methodism and an exciting journey into a hope-filled future that it entails.

Second, this book is also for the 80 or more percent who decide to remain in The United Methodist Church. Though there is still disinformation about United Methodism and Wesleyan thought to correct, we are indeed tired of debate. We are more interested in vision-casting and living into God's future for the United Methodist way of life. So this book is more than a rebuttal to *Multiplying Methodism*, although it is organized in this way. More than a reaction; this response is proactive and creative. This book leans more into the future of what Methodism can and should become than bending in the direction of unresolved conflicts. For those of you, then, who did not entertain the idea of leaving, or struggled and decided to remain, this book is particularly for you. It provides a vision, therefore, that is honest—reforming what is amiss—and grateful—celebrating and strengthening what is right. Our prayer is that of Dag Hammarskjöld: "For all that has been, THANKS; for all that is to be, YES!"[1]

About the Author

If you cut me, I bleed Methodist. I'm a third-generation Methodist minister, not by inheritance but by choice. Methodist clergy (including my spouse) and active lay relatives in my extended family have filled my days with their stories of faith. I love The United Methodist Church and have poured much of my energy into its renewal. As a Wesley scholar my primary concern has always been to restore the Wesleys' vision. The spirit of Methodism and its practical theology will always be more important to me than institutional structures and polity. The Wesleyan vision and spirit inspire me. They call us onward and upward. This tradition that I love is much larger than most people realize, and I have been privileged to love and work with Methodists on three continents.

My teaching career began at Wesley College in Bristol, England, the land of our origins, and ended at Wesley House in Cambridge. Janet and I served in Kenya and helped launch Africa University in Zimbabwe. In the United States, I've tried to help the congregations I pastored to rediscover the Wesleyan way. I pray that the hundreds of students I've taught—in seminaries as diverse as the Methodist Theological School in Ohio and Asbury Theological Seminary in Florida, Ashland Theological Seminary and Duke Divinity School— have fallen in love with our Wesleyan heritage in my classroom. I love Methodism.

Charles Wesley has probably exerted a greater influence on me than his older brother, John. I'm a singer. Charles's amazing ability to translate the faith into lyrical theology, therefore, simply captured me. But I've spent much of my life studying both founders of the Methodist movement. These two brothers oriented their theology— the entirety of their lives, in fact—around the central practice of love. Nothing was more important to them than singing, preaching, and sharing love, God's love known in Christ. Their movement of renewal in the church was a rediscovery of God's unconditional love.

We Love Because God First Loved Us

Our world needs love. It always has and always will. History moves forward in spirals, so once again there seems to be something more desperate about these days of radical polarization and anxiety. Little love is lost between so many nations and peoples. We divide states and communities into red and blue. The ugly resurgence of racism creates deadly chasms in our common life. Christians fight Christians, and the world clamors, "Where's the love?" Even those places we would expect or hope to find love—like the church—seem to have replaced it with an ideology of winning or surviving. Regardless, we are far from hopeless because we believe love is the most powerful reality in this universe. We have a lot of work—a lot of loving—to do.

We are less concerned about the multiplication of Methodisms as we are invested in the multiplication of love that transforms the world. Love is the source, means, and goal; Methodism is a vehicle. We long for the church to be a sanctuary for love in our broken world. We pray the world will look at the church and say, "Oh my. How they love one another!" If Jesus is at the very core of Christian communities, we cannot imagine anything other than love at the very center of our common life.

We need a "gracious" witness more than we need a "bold" witness. The distinction is more about a "Wesleyan way" than a "Wesleyan faith." This vision for the continuing United Methodist Church is dynamic, not static. It commits more to a united witness to God's love than to the codification of a set of beliefs. The "faith" is important; "hope" is important; "love" is more important.

While en route on an arduous journey, division has been hard and painful. In the context of this struggle, with a lot of grief oozing from it, we open our hearts to what God can do and is doing with us in a "post-disaffiliation" state of the Church. Disaffiliation describes those who have left United Methodism, but perhaps more importantly, it characterizes those who have left the faith, those who are now the "nones" and "dones." Rather than "making a stand," especially toward those who walked away from our failures to love, we change our hearts and extend an invitation that offers God's great vision and gift of love to all.

A collect from the *Book of Common Prayer* continues to shape our thinking about the Christian life and the mandate to follow the way of Jesus. It is Wesleyan to the core.

> Lord Jesus Christ, you stretched out your arms of love on the hard wood of the cross that everyone might come within the reach of your saving embrace: So clothe us in your Spirit that we, reaching forth our hands in love, may bring those who do not know you to the knowledge and love of you; for the honor of your Name. Amen.[2]

This prayer celebrates a God with a wide embrace, known to us most fully in the life, death, and resurrection of Jesus. We welcome the image of a God reaching out to take everyone into that loving embrace. But the prayer reminds us, as well, that we are called to imitate Christ. As ambassadors of reconciliation, we have a ministry of reaching out, welcoming, and embracing. This, in fact, is one of the main ways in which the world comes to know this God of love— through us.

We live, unfortunately, in an age of restrictive walls and combative wills. People often seem to be more concerned about being right than cultivating loving relationships with people who are different or who disagree. Rather than reaching out, we all too often hold the "other" at arm's length. We place ourselves in some kind of defensive or superior posture. In my book on *Active Faith*, we observe how this othering reaches into the life of the church. Instead of offering a place in which people can experience healing, we reflect the brokenness that surrounds us. We want to be understood, rather than to understand, as St. Francis taught us. We lose our sense of what is most important—our calling to "be love" in the world for Christ's sake. John Wesley describes this syndrome as losing our first love. The consequence of this shift away from the centrality of humble love is death. When we stop loving, the church dies. I think this is the besetting problem of the church in America. We have lost the ability to proclaim and live love.

The British Methodist hymn writer, Fred Pratt Green, sings about the church of Christ in every age needing to "rise from the dead." When we displace love from the center of our life together, something radical must happen, and God is ready to supply what we need. Resurrection and renewal are always about the rediscovery of love. Our battles in The United Methodist Church these past years left us wounded. Each wound represents a little death. But love always triumphs over death. That is the message of the gospel, the good news of our Lord's resurrection. The prayer, therefore, is for God to multiply love in our family, for us and for the sake of the world, and this implies church renewal.

In teaching about the history of the church, I often use a common contrast to describe different approaches to church. On one hand are those who view the church as a "society of saints." In their view, we have a responsibility to keep the church pure. Obviously, if this is the case, someone must determine what purity means, who is pure, and how to maintain it. Typically, a particular approach to scripture, a Christian doctrine, or an established practice become the measures of purity. We can sense the immediate dangers in selected preferences for purity. On the other hand are those who think of the church as a "school for sinners." Leaders in this school acknowledge the ways in which all of us have sinned. They welcome all, and then provide a means of growing in love and grace toward holiness of heart and life.

A call to holiness has always been a central theme in our Methodist tradition. What makes holiness in the Wesleyan way unique, however, is its clear emphasis on a *holiness of love*—love of God and love of neighbor. Other traditions have often defined holiness in terms of adherence to the law or particular instructions, but this is not the Wesleyan vision. Holiness is all about love. We need to find ways to multiply God's love in our communities and offer God's love freely to others. What if The United Methodist Church were to establish a reputation as the most loving community in the United States and around the world? What if love were our hallmark? What if the first word that came to everyone's mind when they hear the word *Methodist* is *love*? This is our vision—grand as it is—and this is the purpose of this book.

Parallel to *Multiplying Methodism*, by Jeff and Mike, *Multiplying Love* sorts into two sections. The first section focuses on the importance of love and unity in a renewed United Methodist Church (a present need). My response to the situation we face as a church community stands in stark contrast to their rationale for separation. As they focus steadfastly on the "why" of separation, I intend to provide a compelling rationale for unity-in-diversity in the church. The second section of *Multiplying Love* develops a vision of the renewed, inclusive Wesleyan movement of love (a future hope).

The rebuttal rhetoric of a book like this—framed as separation vs. unity, faith vs. love, challenge vs. opportunity—might feel binary, posed as an either/or analysis. It feels uncomfortable for some of us who don't like the dialectic structure of a debate, in part because the local decisions are in practice more complicated (sometimes by self-interest) in each congregation and leader. Regardless, the choice to leave or remain is binary, and I have made my best effort to cultivate an irenic tone. The rebuttal doesn't try to inflict pain or further alienate siblings in Christ. In my responses, therefore, to Jeff and Mike's book (which I can't assume has been read by my own readers), my intention is 1) to be charitable, fair, and honest about their own perspectives and ideas, and 2) to facilitate genuine mutual understanding. But the fact remains that we have (at least) two different visions of the Wesleyan way.

The Wesleyan way is first and foremost a way of love. No one captured this more fully than Charles Wesley in his hymns. He encapsulates his hope, his vision, and his dream in the following hymn. I invite you to make it our own.

> To love is all my wish,
> I only live for this:
> Grant me, Lord, my heart's desire,
> there by faith forever dwell.
> This I always will require,
> thee and only thee to feel.
>
> Thy power I pant to prove
> rooted and fixed in love,
> strengthened by thy Spirit's might,
> wise to fathom things divine.
> What the length and breadth and height,
> what the depth of love like thine.[3]

Part I

Love and Unity in a Renewed United Methodist Church

1

Always Renewing

Don't remember the prior things;
  don't ponder ancient history.
Look! I'm doing a new thing;
  now it sprouts up; don't you recognize it?
I'm making a way in the desert,
  paths in the wilderness. (Isaiah 43:18-19)

Semper fi. Most readers recognize this truncated motto of the United States Marine Corps: *Semper fidelis.* Always faithful, always loyal. In the life of the church—particularly in our Protestant wing—we have our own motto: *Semper reformanda.* Always reforming, always renewing. Karl Barth popularized this abbreviated form of *Ecclesia semper reformanda est.* It reminds us that the church is perennially "on the move" and must constantly attend to its faithfulness to God's way. But it must find new ways of doing things and live its life in constantly changing settings. This frequently means that "we have to change in order to stay the same."

Magrey deVega, during the Florida annual conference, reminded us of this important truth.

> The great orthodox theologian Jaroslav Pelikan asked the question in this way, in a lecture titled, "Does the Church Have to Change in Order to Remain the Same?" The compelling and surprising answer throughout history is, "Yes." The Church has often had to change in its views of personhood, not merely to acquiesce to cultural pressures, but to keep up with the consistent expansiveness and inclusivity of God's love. The Church has changed its views on the inclusion of non-Jews, on slavery, on racial inequity, on the equality of men and women, and on divorce, in order to stay the same in its theology of God's widening hospitality and love.[4]

Methodists are in one of those moments: *Semper ref.*

The opening chapter in *Multiplying Methodism* is entitled, "The Presenting Symptom." The authors argue that, in the ongoing United Methodist debate, the issue of human sexuality is only the "presenting symptom" of much deeper and significant theological differences in the life of the church. Because of these differences, they believe we have reached an impasse that necessitates separation. They devote nearly the entire problem statement, however, to a discussion of the presenting symptom, by articulating their perspective on human sexuality through biblical, theological, pastoral, and secular lenses.

There's no need to rehearse the well-worn arguments[5] in this debate. Most church leaders have a sense about where the divisions lie in terms of the contested biblical material. But there are several points about scripture and social science to address for the sake of mutual understanding.

First, it's disingenuous to claim that one Methodism is "biblical" and the other is not. The human sexuality debate revolves around different "interpretations" of scripture. Each participant in the debate (or in life) considers themselves to be "biblical"—and it is unfair if not self-righteous during discernment to caricature siblings in Christ otherwise. Likewise, "culture" plays a major role in all forms of biblical engagement, acknowledged or not. We each see and understand things through our own cultural lenses. It is unwise, therefore, to separate Christianity and culture too neatly, or to dismiss an opposing view "as reflecting the culture around us" (p. 21), as if that is an automatic disqualifier. Life is not that simple. The introduction of this cultural element segues into a third point, the illustration of which requires more discussion.

How you marshal evidence makes a difference. Jeff and Mike use a very famous study by J. D. Unwin on "Sex and Culture" to support their argument about the sinful and destructive nature of same-sex practice. This study is to buttress their definition of sin as "choosing something less-than-God's-best" (p. 22). The results of Unwin's study on the relationship between sex and the flourishing of cultures are extremely complex. But three statements are germane and will suffice here: 1) Pre-nuptial chastity was the single-most important factor tied to the flourishing of culture. 2) The primary factors securing the *most* flourishing cultures were "pre-nuptial chastity" and "absolute monogamy." 3) Increased sexual freedom leads to the collapse of civilization.

On the basis of Unwin's findings, Jeff and Mike conclude that "when the dominant practice was monogamy and fidelity in heterosexual marriage, the civilization flourished likely because of the strong family unit" (p. 23). Problems abound all around with their articulation of Unwin's findings.

1) Unwin's purpose was to evaluate the proposition that

restraints on sexual activity led to the sublimation of sexual into social energy. Sexually restrained cultures thrive (reach the highest "rationalistic" state of civilization) because humans (Unwin meant males) are forced to divert their sexual energy into other productive channels. Unwin argued from 86 cultures that emancipation of women, which erodes monogamy, always causes a society to fail. This sensibility has nothing to do with the "presenting issue" in United Methodism.

2) "Absolute monogamy" is extremely difficult to maintain and has only ever been established, according to Unwin, by the subjugation of women to their husbands. A host of ethical issues swirl around this conclusion.

3) The Unwin study makes no reference to "absolute *heterosexual* monogamy," no mention of strong or weak "family units." These ideas are simply imposed on Unwin's conclusions. Their implication is that non-heterosexual marriages and families lead to decay.

4) Most significantly, this study was conducted in 1934, nearly a century ago, and there is no reference within it to "homosexual" or "same-sex" practices or activities. In other words, no conclusions can be drawn from the Unwin study that apply to the same-sex "realities" of our own time.

With regard to what Jeff and Mike describe as the presenting symptom (failure to obey the scripture regarding sexual behavior), there's not enough space here for rehashing the debate, but let's return to the "Pelikan principle" described above: Sometimes we Methodists must change to remain the same. In fact, we have changed our perspective on the interpretation of many matters in scripture by applying a Wesleyan interpretive lens.

Three principles of biblical interpretation embedded in our

Methodist DNA are of importance in this regard. These are significant, as we will explore more fully later, because different understandings of scripture and how the Bible functions within the community of faith are critical forces leading to division.

1. *The whole tenor of scripture.* Particular texts in the Bible must be measured against the whole—the larger narrative and pervasive themes—to make sure our interpretation is aligned with God's loving purposes.
2. *Scripture vis-à-vis scripture.* Difficult texts must be laid alongside clear texts to clarify their meaning.
3. *The analogy of Christ.* We must read scripture through the loving eyes of Christ. He becomes the measure of all things in terms of the meaning of biblical texts.

There are many examples of how John Wesley changed his understanding of scriptural texts on the basis of these principles. His changed view of women in ministry is an illustration. Initially Wesley held firmly to a "traditionalist" interpretation of the so-called prohibitive passages in Paul's New Testament writings alluding to women. Flatly, Wesley prohibited women from preaching in the same way he prohibited lay preaching in general. But when he witnessed the preaching of women and discerned their spiritual gifts and the fruit of their ministry, he felt compelled to revisit those texts. He changed his view of scripture on the basis of his experience. He didn't abandon the Bible; he embraced a new understanding of difficult texts.

Thereafter he justified the public role of women on the basis of other biblical texts (Acts 2:17-18; Romans 16; Galatians 3:28) that superseded the purported prohibitions. He accepted the ministry of women because of their transparent devotion to and love of God so closely aligned with God's way. He viewed women through the eyes of Christ; their faithfulness and success proved the validity of their calling and labor. Suffice it to say, he changed (altered his interpretation of texts) in order to stay the same (give priority to his partnership with God in God's mission of love in the world).

Changes of perspective like this always hinge on a reassessment of scripture because we take the Bible seriously and wish to be in sync with God's vision in all things. The Wesleys viewed this kind of biblical engagement and the transformation it entails as a critical aspect of their faithfulness. This kind of Wesleyan biblical engagement must be applied to the participation of lesbian, gay, bisexual, and transgender participants who bring their spiritual gifts and the fruit of their ministry into Christian communities. I testify that a close study of the handful of texts—none of which really address contemporary issues related to sexuality but are tangential to them—changed my perspective along with millions of others.

Here are writ-large conclusions:[6]

- *Creation or Re-creation.* God created all that is out of love. God loves all that God created. Despite the brokenness that characterizes our individual lives and our human family, God is at work to restore love's image in our lives through a process of re-creation. God wills that we reach out to others in love. Love is every person's reason for being.

- *Covenant.* God makes covenants with people that provide a structure for redemption. The biblical conception of covenant as it relates to our most intimate relationships in life is characterized by sacredness; fidelity; permanency, and monogamy. These characteristics apply to all sexual relationships, regardless of their nature. God seeks to infuse these qualities into all relationships of love.

- *God's Reign.* Everything moves ultimately toward the realization of God's rule in all things. Justice, peace, harmony, and love—shalom—characterize God's mission. Under the rule of God, all persons are free to embrace and employ their unique gifts in partnership with God. Every person has a role to play in God's restoration of all things.

With regard to siblings in the queer* segment of our Christian or human family, scripture reveals three things in particular. 1) All people, regardless of their sexual orientation or identity, are dearly loved by God. Love is their reason for being, and this is the case for all God's children. 2) Relationships based on love among our queer siblings can be expressed in sacredness, fidelity, permanency, and monogamy. These high standards apply to all those created in the image of God. 3) As beloved children of God, all queer siblings are invited to use their gifts to the fullest possible extent in the embodiment of God's vision of shalom. Just as in the case of women, the doors to ministry in the life of the church should be opened to these faithful siblings as well.

When Jeff and Mike state that "the Bible tells us God's best, when it comes to the good gift of our human sexuality is monogamy and fidelity (exclusive faithfulness) in the marriage of a man and a

---

* The word *queer* used here is an umbrella term for persons who identify or prefer not to identify their sexuality as lesbian, gay, bisexual, transgender, queer, intersex, or asexual.

woman and celibacy (abstinence from sex) in singleness" (pp. 23-4), a super-majority of Methodists agree wholeheartedly—with exception made for the phrase "in the marriage of a man and a woman." Our study of scripture, our personal experiences with siblings in the non-heteronormative world, and a deep desire to partner with God in God's mission have led most of us to a wider embrace. We had to change opinions about whom we love in order to remain the same concerning God's love for all.

We have been engaged in thinking together about the human-sexuality-divide as the presenting symptom—the tip of the iceberg of deeper divisions in Jeff and Mike's view—that necessitates separation. Let's turn this narrative around. It's much more interesting to use the need for spiritual renewal as the presenting issue; as the basis of a greater and unifying need. Let's seize this moment of division as an opportunity for renewal in The United Methodist Church. Most certainly, as a church we are at a tipping point. Wise leaders tend to say, "Never waste a good crisis."

From my point of view, we have long abandoned our passion for renewal. Without doubt, Jeff and Mike would agree. In part, renewal is a stated (more wholistic) motivation for why some among us prefer to leave.

Renewal is a thread woven throughout the course of this book. Most of the time it will be an undercurrent, but every now and then it will rise to the surface. When it does somewhat organically, we can talk together about what it looks like. Here it would be helpful simply to pause to ask the question, How does God renew the church? What is the new thing God is doing right now?

The prophet Isaiah triggers our approach.

Don't remember the prior things;
   don't ponder ancient history.
Look! I'm doing a new thing;
   now it sprouts up; don't you recognize it? (43:18-19a)

United Methodists know that it's time to move on. While embroiled in the relational turmoil and dealing with our grief, this doesn't mean we close our eyes or put our head in the sand. Rather, it means we shift attention to the new creation that God is enacting before our very eyes. Is God gifting us with a new vision of radical inclusion in the life of the church? That's how it feels to many. How might this be healing? Can we celebrate the joy of new life in this new thing that God is doing? Now it sprouts! Don't you see it?

We have some sense of Isaiah's feeling when he looked forward. He uses two common biblical words to describe it: *wilderness* and *desert*. Those are not happy places. In my mind they conjure up images of hunger, thirst, loneliness, exhaustion, and desperation. Have you been there? Are you there now? But in those very places in our lives and in the life of the church God makes a way and offers living water in the form of a river (43:19).

In the following pages about the power of love, think about the joy we experience when all are included. Let's sing a new song about the renewing activity of the Spirit that leads to peace with justice, healing with hope, joy with love.

2

Love Is the Highest Gift

If I have the gift of prophecy and I know all the mysteries and everything else, and if I have such complete faith that I can move mountains but I don't have love, I'm nothing. . . .

Now we see a reflection in a mirror; then we will see face-to-face. Now I know partially, but then I will know completely in the same way that I have been completely known. Now faith, hope, and love remain—these three things—and the greatest of these is love. (1 Corinthians 13:2, 12-13)

Doctrine matters. What we believe shapes who we are and all we do. The agenda of the very first conference of Wesley's traveling preachers in 1744 revolved around three questions. What do we teach? was the first, followed by How do we teach? and What do we do? After forty years teaching Methodist doctrine, I'm passionate about reclaiming Wesleyan theology because it is as relevant and unique today as it was in the time of the Methodist revival.

It is harmful to drive a wedge between our faith and our life—between what we believe and how we live. The two are integrally connected. Charles Wesley loved singing about faith. Faith pervades his hymns:

> Author of faith, eternal Word,
>   whose Spirit breathes the active flame;
> faith, like its finisher and Lord,
>   today as yesterday the same.

> To thee our humble hearts aspire,
>   and ask the gift unspeakable:
> Increase in us the kindled fire,
>   in us the work of faith fulfil.[7]

The Wesleys talked about "faith" in two distinct senses. They distinguish between the "faith in which one believes" (*fides quae creditur*) and the "faith by which one believes" (*fides qua creditur*). The Latin phrases emerged from the Reformation. The former could be described as faith in the sense of a "belief system," or simply "belief." It is THE faith (once delivered to the saints), objective statements about "what" you believe. The Wesleys contrast this systematic faith with subjective faith, also described as "living" or "saving faith." Whereas belief tends to be intellectual knowledge, a construct of the mind, this kind of saving faith is a matter of the heart. There is a dynamic, relational quality to living faith; belief appears more static or fixed. Both kinds of faith, knowledge of God and love of God (contrasted by the prophet Hosea) are important. The Wesleys, as you might expect however, always placed a person's experience of faith (love of God and neighbor) above what they might claim to believe.

The second chapter of *Multiplying Methodism*, "Contending for the Faith," is about faith as doctrines or statements we believe. It is more about belief as knowledge than faith as love. The central theme of their chapter is "the problem of doctrinal drift from the core of the Christian faith" (p. 37). Jeff and Mike consider this deviation from "orthodoxy" to be so substantial that it can be tolerated no longer. The "presenting symptom" of different perspectives on human sexuality (discussed in the previous chapter), lays bare much deeper doctrinal divisions in their view.

They identify five areas of "disagreement over what constitutes fidelity to the historic confessions of the Christian faith" (p. 32):

- the nature, role, and authority of scripture
- the nature, role, and authority of Jesus
- the nature of and remedy for human sin
- the meaning of justification/salvation
- and the meaning of Christian sanctification.

In these significant arenas of theological concern, they seek to contend for "the very heart of the Christian faith" (p. 32). Obviously, this is serious business!

Jeff and Mike identify the adoption of theological pluralism by the United Methodist General Conference of 1972 (the same year debate emerges concerning homosexuality) as the source of "heresy" or "diseased Christianity" in our denomination. To support their claims about doctrinal slippage, they provide three anecdotal illustrations of aberrant teachings on the Trinity, Atonement, and Christology on the part of church leaders, and they identify three United Methodist seminaries that reflect these dangerous tendencies. They draw a threefold strategy from the book of Jude in their effort to contend for the faith: 1) Declare allegiance to Jesus Christ as Lord, 2) face reality (resist "false teaching" as the greatest threat to the heart of the gospel), and 3) reclaim Christian orthodoxy.

An indirect response to Jeff and Mike's concerns is more appropriate than an attempt to tackle these complex issues head on. Their concern about doctrinal drift in United Methodism opens the door for a larger conversation about the purpose and goals of theology in our tradition. The main concern rests not in their critique of contemporary Methodist theology. We could go round and round on our differences here—and not change the trajectory of our witness and effectiveness. The problem with their approach has to do with the way they privilege "doctrine" and seem to view a return to doctrinal purity as the antidote for the decline of influence through the Christian faith today. Two critical aspects of Wesleyan theology shed light on a way forward in this regard: 1) theology as transformation and 2) love as "the sum of all."

The purpose of theology is transformation, not safeguarding orthodoxy in the sense of getting doctrine right. John Wesley distinguished between "practical" and "speculative divinity." He realized that there were many aspects of theology in which speculation helps no one. As you surely know, Christians have spilled the blood of other Christians over differences of opinion with regard to unanswerable questions. That is painful, but it is true. Wesley decided not to spend his time speculating about concerns that made no measurable difference in people's lives. He was a practical, not a speculative theologian. This endeared him to the people, particularly to those for whom this "theological world" was a totally alien sphere.

For this very reason, Wesley determined to speak "plain words for plain people."[8] This is why his primary mode of theological expression was the sermon. He had the uncanny ability to simplify, synthesize, and communicate the essential teachings of the Christian gospel (note that he was far from indifferent to doctrine in this sense) so common people could understand and be transformed by them. He inherited "confessions of faith" and "creeds" that articulated the fundamentals of the Christian faith, but he did not view adherence or intellectual assent to these statements as the most essential aspect of his mission, regardless of their importance.

Likewise, Charles sang the faith. He dedicated theology to the service of transformation as well. More heavily reliant on the language of scripture than the explanation of it, he packaged the good news of God's love in poetry. When people sang his hymns, they felt the love of God—"love divine, all loves excelling"—in their hearts. For him theology was meant to transform our dispositions and desires, enabling us to take on the mind of Christ and the fruit of the Spirit. The Wesleys' preaching and singing transformed the lives of countless people who longed to know a God who loved them.

Most Methodists are extremely dubious about how doctrinal purity along the lines that Jeff and Mike prescribe will lead to renewal in the church. I'm a theologian, so I hold these doctrinal nuances close as the rhetoric of my profession. But many factors beyond "bad theology" swirl around the demise and influence of Christendom in the Western world. Having served on Boards of Ordained Ministry, I observed how, when asked to articulate their understanding of the Trinity, many worthy and promising candidates wavered and even fell into the pitfalls of ancient "heretical" views. Efforts to provide an intellectual explanation about the meaning of the cross often elude the most diligent of students. In an essay on the Wesleys' view of the person and work of Christ for a volume on *Methodist Christology*, I employed the language of "practical Christology." I wrote this about my students' perspective regarding doctrinal matters:

> To state it rather bluntly, they can discern the practical "so what?" factor related to a disproportional emphasis on either Jesus's humanity or his divinity. But speculative attempts to explain the natures' interrelationship leave my students without clear practical guidance for their journey into the fullest possible love of God and neighbor. I sense a similar disposition of mind and heart in the Wesleys.[9]

Perhaps this is why the church has never established dogmatic declarations about atonement (which is a made-up word, at-one-ment, devised by Tyndale in the 1500s). None of these speculations are new. It simply reflects the difficulty of giving intellectual expression to the mysteries of the faith. We see reflections dimly in a mirror.

At some point, the struggle to understand or articulate the mystery loses its transformational power. Despite these challenges, very few Methodists have "abandoned Christ." The vast majority testify willingly to the healing and liberation they've experienced through Jesus Christ as the Lord of their lives. They praise the persons of the Trinity, not because this explains God but because they cannot remain silent, as St. Augustine observed.

When John Wesley attempted to describe "The Character of a Methodist" (1742),[10] he began by telling the reader what a Methodist is not. The distinguishing marks of the Methodist, he observed, are not a peculiar set of opinions, notions, doctrines, actions, or customs. Methodists are those, Wesley claims, who have "the love of God shed abroad in their hearts by the Holy Ghost given unto them" (see Romans 5:5): those who "love the Lord their God with all their heart, and with all their soul, and with all their mind, and with all their strength" (see Mark 12:30). The Wesleys' purpose was spiritual renewal—a rediscovery of faith working by love.

A theology did undergird their efforts and beliefs, to be sure, and it quickly took on a normative character. Over time, formative expressions of Methodist theology further defined this theological inheritance. Multiple historical and cultural contexts shaped and reshaped it as the movement expanded, literally, around the globe. This complexity has enriched our understanding of God and expanded our vision of how to live in this world. As embodied in the ministry of E. Stanley Jones, a posture of openness—openness to different truths, cultures, contexts, voices—gives us strength. The purpose of transformation reminds us that faith must be translated into action, bringing about purposeful change, growth, and restoration. This posture and this purpose facilitate renewal.

Love is "the sum of all" when it comes to Christian doctrine. John Wesley often distinguished "essential" Christian beliefs from what he described as "opinions."[11] In his general use of these terms, the former he views as critical to the life of faith, shaping its foundations and its goals; the latter are allowable but only marginally significant. He acknowledges, in other words, that there is a hierarchy of belief, and it helps us in our journey of faith toward deeper love to have clarity about what is most important and what is not.

To put a singular issue right up front, most Methodists have never considered human sexuality (or a person's gendered identity) an essential issue with regard to matters of faith. We don't consider one's perspective on sexuality to be a cause, therefore, for division. Sexual identity falls into the category of opinion, not essential Christian belief—which is apparently why some Methodists are so uncomfortable with our queer siblings that they overreach to shift their opposition into calcified theological controversies about biblical authority, Christology, and atonement.

While sexuality isn't a just cause for church division among us Methodists, this doesn't minimize the importance of sexuality in our lives. Our whole identity is bound inextricably with our self-understanding in this regard. How could it not be critical? So, while not wanting to minimize its importance, I must acknowledge simultaneously that one's view on human sexuality is not essential to the creeds for the Christian faith. This is simply to say that where we draw the line between essentials and opinions is the question with which we struggle today. Wesley can provide some guidance.

Wesley's list of essentials varies widely depending on his context. The list expands or contracts on the basis of the issue at hand. Typically, his essentials revolve around the "way of salvation." In his "Principles of a Methodist Farther Explained," for example, he classically asserts, "Our main doctrines, which include all the rest, are three, that of repentance, of faith, and of holiness. The first of these we account, as it were, the porch of religion; the next, the door; the third, religion itself."[12] There are longer lists than this, but it is the three doctrines embedded in this statement—original sin, justification by grace through faith, and sanctification—that figure most frequently and prominently.[13] But even with regard to these, in "A Plain Account of the People called Methodists," he claims: "Orthodoxy, or right opinions, is at best but a slender part of religion, if it can be allowed to be a part at all."[14]

Are there no essentials at all? More importantly, if orthodox doctrine is not a fixed foundation for our Christian life, then what is religion? What is the essence of our life in God?

First John 4:19—"We love because God first loved us"—was a formative biblical text for both John and Charles Wesley. It figures prominently in John's preaching and Charles's hymns. In his reflections on this text in his *Explanatory Notes on the New Testament*, John Wesley writes, "This is the sum of all religion, the genuine model of Christianity. None can say more: why should anyone say less?" The most important thing, in other words, is the experience of God's love, living in the love of Christ, and sharing that love freely with others. Nothing is more essential than love; it is the sum of all things.

In his sermon on the Trinity, he makes this claim even more boldly:

> Whatsoever the generality of people may think, it is certain that opinion is not religion: no, not right opinion; assent to one or to ten thousand truths. There is a wide difference between them: even right opinion is as distant from religion as the east is from the west. Persons may be quite right in their opinions, yet have no religion at all. And on the other hand, persons may be truly religious who hold many wrong opinions . . . but many of them are now real Christians, loving God and all mankind.[15]

Wesley's perspective on truth (doctrine) and love is very clear. Beliefs really are important, so long as they lead the believer in the way of love. But love, in and of itself, is even more valuable than Christian belief. All Christian doctrines and practices must be brought under the scrutiny of God's love for us and God's expectation that we extend that love to everyone. All is gift, but love is the highest gift.

3

Why We Need to Embrace Unity

Therefore, as a prisoner for the Lord, I encourage you to live as people worthy of the call you received from God. Conduct yourselves with all humility, gentleness, and patience. Accept each other with love, and make an effort to preserve the unity of the Spirit with the peace that ties you together. You are one body and one spirit, just as God also called you in one hope. There is one Lord, one faith, one baptism, and one God and Father of all, who is over all, through all, and in all. (Ephesians 4:1-6)

The Holy Spirit fosters unity. But unity is elusive. In a circulating letter to the Ephesians, the writer pleads, begs for Christians to rise up to their high calling to live as a united community of faith. To do this requires humility, gentleness, patience, and loving tolerance. Let's affirm the phrase, "the unity of the Spirit with the peace that ties you together." Both these virtues, unity and peace, are products of life guided by the Spirit of Christ. This is evident in that long string of "ones": one body, one spirit, one hope, one Lord, one faith, one baptism, one God. You almost want to say, "Is anyone confused?" How could the apostle make it clearer? God's call to unity is one of the most critical aspects of who we are called to be as God's people, as the family of Jesus.

Yet we are all different, aren't we? And our differences frequently become barriers in our quest for unity. We all know intuitively that this unity must be a unity-in-diversity. There is no other form of unity available to us. Even God's unity is a unity-in-diversity. It is a unity-in-relationship. Father to Son; Son to Spirit; Spirit to Father. A glorious circle of oneness—a celebration of unity-in-diversity. And we are no different. Like God, we are diverse, but we are united by love. Love is the essence of our unity. Unity is possible for us because, as Paul says, God "is over all, through all, and in all."

But life requires that we draw lines, doesn't it? Issues of inclusion and exclusion are never easy. Because of our brokenness, there are some forces that disrupt and even destroy unity. Sin (selfish desire) causes division. In order to restore unity, when people are torn apart by fear or animosity or deliberate action, only reconciliation can restore peace and unity in our lives. This is the hard work of love in a broken world. But this is also the hope of the Christian community because Christ has made all forms of reconciliation possible through his death and resurrection.

As we've seen, most division in the life of the church involves different understandings about what lines need to be drawn and where. We must make decisions as a community, therefore, about this matter on the basis of our understanding of scripture, just as we did in the past with regard to slavery and women in ministry. As is often the case, our different ways of interpreting scripture led us to different conclusions. Like Luther and Zwingli at the famous Marburg Colloquy, the great reformers agreed on fourteen critical areas of doctrine, but they disagreed on one. That disagreement split them into two different traditions, Lutheran and Reformed. Splitting over one out of fifteen essential doctrines is a tragic example of stubbornness. There is a better way; not easier—but better.

In chapter 3 of Jeff and Mike's book, they outline their rationale for the necessity of separation from The United Methodist Church. They critique "big tent" Methodism as the product of the "theological pluralism" accepted and adopted in the church when it united. For them, the tent was too big, permitting understandings and practices of the faith that fall beyond the lines they have drawn. "We believe separations are sometimes necessary and even justified," they conclude, "if the motivation is for the sake of the mission of making disciples of Jesus Christ" (pp. 48-49). In an effort to explain this decision, they turn to a familiar story related to mission in the earliest church.

They argue that Paul and Barnabas, two of the early church's greatest missionaries, went their separate ways instead of jeopardizing the mission of the nascent church. A difference of opinion fractured their relationship and set them on different paths. They contend, as well, that we are at a Paul-and-Barnabas moment today in The United Methodist Church. The differences inside the church have become so pronounced that remaining together potentially harms our mission in the world.

They offer then six reasons why separation is necessary:

1. We are no longer governable.
2. We have language problems.
3. We have very different theologies.

4. We don't want to be in the same church.
5. We're hurting each other.
6. We need to start planting.

With regard to the theological differences, they rehearse again the five primary concerns raised in their previous chapter that revolve around scripture, Christology, sin, salvation, and sanctification.

After responding to the way in which Jeff and Mike frame the issue of separation, we examine their rationale for this action before proactively making a case for unity. While at first glance the separation of Paul and Barnabas in the mission fields of Asia Minor might seem to have parallels to our own situation, the first century really doesn't apply to the twenty-first century. Barnabas's disagreement with Paul did not touch upon the essentials of the faith; rather, it was a difference of opinion with regard to strategy and personnel. Moreover, the church at that nascent stage hardly represented something we could describe as a denomination. They were not splintering a church, as is the case with United Methodism today. Their personal circumstances simply don't provide insight or guidance for a denomination which, in Jeff and Mike's words, "has lost its way" (p. 50). It simply doesn't help us move forward, which is the direction we would prefer to take.

Secondly, without question, "the Church is a movement fueled and driven by the Holy Spirit" (p. 46), but the Spirit of Christ doesn't fuel or drive separation. (We will address this more fully in the next chapter.) The Spirit unites; it doesn't divide. When Luther parted from Zwingli at Marburg, fracturing the Protestant movement, his final words were purportedly, "We are not of the same spirit." While that ego wound has never been fully healed, conversations in past years have brought much healing and deeper understanding between the two communities. Repentance has been offered from each side to the other with a recognition that this division was "not a good thing." It wasn't driven by the Holy Spirit but by a spirit refusing to embrace the idea that faithful Christians can come to different conclusion about the same texts of scripture.

There is no need to respond to every reason for separation identified by our friends who have left. Several issues here, however, arise that factor into a different vision of unity. First, with regard to the issue of "a language problem," this dissonance has always been true within the community of faith from its very beginnings. Language and word choice will always be in play as faithful Christians enter the perilous process of "translating" the faith into new cultural contexts and, literally, languages. We are called to listen intently and patiently for the purpose of mutual understanding. Some feel they have listened long enough. My fear is that on all sides of a debate about words we never listen enough.

They also make the claim that "we have very different theologies" (pp. 51-52). Agreed. Do not mourn; let's celebrate this! In a survey of "Methodist Theology" for the *St. Andrew's University Encyclopaedia of Theology,* I identify the various streams of theology in our Methodist tradition. Everything begins, of course, with a distinctive and well-defined headwater in the "practical theology" of John and Charles Wesley. New streams emerged from within this "living stream," as well they should, as Methodists (all within the lineage of the Wesleys) responded to the changing and challenging terrain of the following centuries. Theologies described as holiness, liberal (including Boston personalism, the social gospel, and process theology), neo-Wesleyan (in two distinct patterns), and contextual theologies (including black and womanist, liberation and feminist, and indigenous theologies) have all played a role in bringing the gospel to life in different contexts. Our theology represents a unity-in-diversity of its own, and this holy conversation is something we need to celebrate, neither lament nor suppress.

The extent to which any of these streams remains faithful to the original vision of the Wesleys depends on several factors. Our United Methodist doctrinal standards, of course, must figure prominently as we adjudicate these kinds of questions. The following statement summarizes our approach:

> Methodists do not view these standards and landmark documents as a system of formal theology to be imposed on the church in dogmatic fashion. They do not understand themselves to be a "confessional" tradition despite their adherence to the Apostles' Creed. Rather, these documents function as standards of preaching and belief which should secure loyalty to the fundamental truths of the gospel of redemption and ensure the continued witness of the church to the realities of the Christian experience of salvation.[16]

This is an important feature of Methodism. How we use doctrine is as important as the doctrine we use. Differences call, most certainly, for a generous broad-mindedness. What can I learn from this other perspective? That is a genuine first-order question. The question—How has this person's or this community's life and theology advanced the causes of God's love?—comes hot on its heels.

In light of this discussion, three simple statements frame a rationale for unity in the current and continuing United Methodist Church. These statements will be explained more fully in a discussion of our Wesleyan heritage, in the next chapter. The first two propositions are biblical; the third is missiological—reflecting our concern about God's mission in our world. A closing comment about the centrality of Eucharist to this rationale concludes the chapter.

Jesus prays for the unity of the church. It is very hard for any Methodist to get around this simple fact. Jesus's high priestly prayer in John 17 demonstrates with amazing clarity just how important the unity of his community across time and space is to him. Jesus prays passionately:

> I'm not praying only for them but also for those who believe in me because of their word. I pray they will be one, Father, just as you are in me and I am in you. I pray that they also will be in us, so that the world will believe that you sent me. I've given them the glory that you gave me so that they can be one just as we are one. I'm in them and you are in me so that they will be made perfectly one. Then the world will know that you sent me and that you have loved them just as you loved me. (John 17:20-23)

Complete unity. That is Jesus's vision for us. John roots the unity of the church in nothing other than God's unity. The primary purpose of unity in the church is "then the world will know."

Paul places unity at the center of our common life. The theme of unity pervades the apostle's writings: Romans 12:16, 1 Corinthians 1:10, 2 Corinthians 13:11, Galatians 3:28, Ephesians 4:3, Philippians 2:2, Colossians 3:14. In these texts we learn that unity requires great effort but brings joy and peace, reflecting the love and peace of God. We particularly appreciate how the Colossians text links love with unity or harmony: "And over all these things put on love, which is the perfect bond of unity" (Colossians 3:14). Perfect unity. That is the Pauline vision for us. Separation in the church, with regard to which scripture says nothing positive, is antithetical to the call to unity.

God's mission requires a united church. The witness of both Jesus and Paul points to the missiological significance of unity. Jesus is explicit about it, praying not once but twice, that we might be "perfectly one" so that "the world will believe that you sent me." Separation puts our mission in serious jeopardy. Our partnership with God in God's mission hangs in the balance. If we have nothing to offer the world other than a legacy of separation, alienation, and division, then we have nothing to offer that the world has not already mastered.

Jesus brings his disciples in close and says, "This is how everyone will know that you are my disciples, when you love each other" (John 13:35). Our unity demonstrates our love for Jesus and for each other. That is the ministry—the high calling—into which God calls us. United in mission. That is God's vision for us.

At the table of the Lord, we live the parable of unity-in-diversity. Our actions proclaim that every person is welcome, every child of God included, all united in one family of love. Jesus made a particular practice of eating with those who were oppressed and excluded by others. He welcomed, accepted, and empowered them to be part of his mission of love in the world.

The table of the Lord—God's great sign-act of love—presents its own irrefutable rationale for unity. "Come to the Supper come," Charles Wesley sings. "Every soul may be his guest."[17] The host excludes no one. At the table all barriers fall to the ground. The Lord feeds us and makes us one. The sacrament demonstrates to everyone why we need to embrace God's gift of unity. All are welcomed and all are loved around the table.

4

The Peaceable Reign of Christ

The wolf will live with the lamb,
and the leopard will lie down with the young goat;
the calf and the young lion will feed together,
and a little child will lead them.
The cow and the bear will graze.
Their young will lie down together,
and a lion will eat straw like an ox.
A nursing child will play over the snake's hole;
toddlers will reach right over the serpent's den.
They won't harm or destroy anywhere on my holy mountain.
The earth will surely be filled with the knowledge of the Lord,
just as the water covers the sea. (Isaiah 11:6-9)

United Methodists have opportunity to pray the following prayer from our hymnal at the beginning of each day:

New every morning is your love, great God of light,
    and all day long you are working for good in the world.
Stir up in us desire to serve you,
    to live peacefully with our neighbors,
and to devote each day to your Son,
    our Savior, Jesus Christ the Lord. Amen.[18]

The vision of God's kingdom embedded in this prayer pervades scripture and constitutes the central teaching of Jesus. Martin Luther King, Jr. described the goal of God's ongoing work through Christ and us in the world as the "beloved community."[19] Walter Bruegge-man identified God's rule with the single Hebrew word *shalom*—a vision of "a caring, sharing, rejoicing community with none to make them afraid."[20]

In a hymn on the incarnation of Christ, Charles Wesley describes God's kingdom as a "quiet and peaceable reign."

All glory to God in the sky,
    and peace upon earth be restored!
O Jesus, exalted on high,
    appear our omnipotent Lord:

Who meanly in Bethlehem born,
    didst stoop to redeem a lost race,
Once more to thy creatures return,
    and reign in thy kingdom of grace.

Come then to thy servants again,
    who long thy appearing to know,
thy quiet and peaceable reign
    in mercy establish below:

All sorrow before thee shall fly,
    and anger and hatred be o'er,

and envy and malice shall die,
and discord afflict us no more.[21]

Grace characterizes this alternative community in the world. When grace, mercy, and love prevail, joy replaces sorrow, love displaces anger and hatred, community supplants envy and malice, and unity and harmony supersede our penchant for discord. God transforms us from a people of noise, rancor, and division into a united family, in which the quiet and peaceable reign of Christ rules. God invites us to live into and to embody this vision. In and through this rule we celebrate diversity, embrace those different from us who also seek to love and to be loved, and offer the gift of restored unity as a gift to the world. Isaiah 11:6-9 provides the primary locus for this iconic vision through which "They won't harm or destroy anywhere on my holy mountain."

This is our high calling. This is the mission to which God calls us. We are God's ambassadors of peace and reconciliation. God calls us to do no harm and to heal. God invites us into a partnership that does good in the world, that unites and does not divide. The Lord of history sets a vision before us—the quiet and peaceable reign of Christ—and enables us to live this vision for the sake of the world, empowered by the Spirit.

In chapter 4 of their book, Jeff and Mike ask two questions: How are people to faithfully follow the Lord of history? and How does the separation taking place align with the history of the Methodist (Wesleyan) movement (pp. 57-58)? They maintain that "Christians are to operate under the rule of the Lord Jesus Christ. He alone is to be our master" (p. 60). But we will see how their vision of what that rule means stands in contrast to the biblical vision. They use the story of

King David in 1 Chronicles 12 to illustrate how "obedience to God's purposes and plans took precedence over their desires and ideas" (p. 61). They interpret the account of the Council of Jerusalem in Acts 15 as an incidence in which Peter didn't seek popularity "or succumb to the lowest common denominator of compromise" (p. 62) but was "faithful and obedient to the Lord of history."[22]

In defense of separation from The United Methodist Church today, they marshal evidence from the history of the church—from the Great Schism between Catholics and Orthodox (1054) to the American (1784) and British (1795) separation of Methodism from the Church of England—in which, in their view, "doctrinal fidelity" superseded "institutional Christian unity." With regard to schisms in the history of Methodism—including those of the African Methodist Episcopal Church, the O'Kelly-founded Republican Methodist Church, the Methodist Protestant Church, the Free Methodist Church, and the schism between the northern and southern branches of the Methodist Episcopal Church—they interpret these divisive events as "God's [creative?] determination to have a fresh and vibrant witness" (p. 65). They describe what is happening in the life of our church today as "a part of a larger process of growth, struggle with doctrinal clarity, and the future of the Wesleyan witness to a larger witness" (p. 65).

In the closing pages of their chapter, they interpret the development of the Holy Club at Oxford and the "open conflict" between John Wesley and George Whitefield as two examples that further support their appeal for separation. Neither of these examples, however, led to division in a church. Rather, the Holy Club represents the "first rise of Methodism," a movement of renewal that remained in the Church of England. The "tensions" between Wesley and

Whitefield led to separation (between two leaders), but not within a church. These two examples reflect nothing parallel to the situation in which we find ourselves today. Ironically, Jeff and Mike turn one of John Wesley's most significant appeals for unity-in-diversity on its head, using his sermon on "the Catholic Spirit" to support their claims that separation is necessary.

As a historian of the church and the Methodist tradition, and as an exegete of Wesleyan theological documents, I simply couldn't disagree more with their analysis or the logic of their argument. Their revisionist view of church history and God's purposes in it turns darkness into light. Instead of viewing schism as a destructive event in Methodism, they embrace division as a tool of God's purposes in the world. Division may be an unintended consequence of our Protestant impulse to transform and change our hearts and minds. But schism and division always move the church in the wrong direction—away from reform, instead toward preserving and conserving the past. Schism is the product of misunderstanding, corporate hubris, and socioeconomic forces that go far beyond concerns for "theological integrity."

Some of the divisions Jeff and Mike affirm as part of "God's creative determination" inflicted deep wounds that are yet to be fully healed. Schism, division, and separation reflect the broken nature of our human and institutional relationships. Far from something to be celebrated, church and heart division should bring us to our knees. As Jesus prayed in John 14, division requires repentance and restoration. The ecumenical efforts of the past century fostered great strides forward in the healing of the divisions between Roman and Orthodox Christians, the Protestant heritage and Rome, and inside many denominations, including our own. Thank God that many

Methodists relinquished the divisive spirit of the nineteenth century and replaced it with a deep desire for unity and restoration.

The Wesleys vehemently opposed all efforts to divide the church in their own day. Their singular quest was for God's reign in broken hearts and in a broken world. They pursued and advocated Christian unity indefatigably. John Wesley demonstrated a severe aversion to "separation" from the Church of England—a direct parallel to the situation in The United Methodist Church today. He guided his followers into the ways of peace and unity through his preaching, publishing, and direct action.

John Wesley's sermon on "the Catholic Spirit" defines his vision of unity-in-diversity in the life of the church. Jeff and Mike argue that this sermon does not advocate indifference with regard to doctrine. Wesley uses statements that could be construed that way. Two are classic: "Though we cannot think alike, may we not love alike" and "If your heart is like my heart, give me your hand." Up to this point I am in sympathy with their conclusion. We need clarity about the "essentials of faith." But our friends go wrong in their isolation of the "doctrinal statements" in the sermon from Wesley's overarching purpose. He doesn't publish this sermon as a clarion call to clarity and fidelity in belief; the purpose of the sermon is to promote a vision of Christian unity despite diversity in theological opinions.

Here are the sermon's primary points.

1. God calls us to love all our siblings in a united family of love.
2. What really matters is having a heart rooted in love, believing in Christ, and filled with the energy of love demonstrated through concrete actions.

3. The love we need to embody is the self-sacrificing love we see in Jesus.
4. We need to take what we believe about essential matters seriously, but never make our own opinions the rule for all.
5. We must enlarge our hearts to all God's children despite our differences. "Catholic Spirit" defends a generous orthodoxy in the service of unity-in-diversity.

It is revealing that Jeff and Mike omit reference to John Wesley's famous treatise, "Reasons against Separation from the Church of England," in their chapter advocating separation from The United Methodist Church. It is disingenuous to ignore such a strong statement about the need for Methodists to remain faithful and loyal to the Anglican Church when so many of Wesley's followers were clamoring for separation. The situation Wesley faced then parallels what we face in our church today. His appeal advocates unequivocal unity in the face of tension and disagreement, theological or otherwise. Both John and Charles Wesley remained devoted priests of the Church of England to their dying day. It isn't too much to say that they refused to listen to any argument for separation or sanctioned any action that compromised the unity of the church.

During the 1750s some of Wesley's preachers increased their agitation for separation from the Church of England. They believed the church was so captive to culture that continued association with it impeded the Methodist mission. At the 1755 Conference John affirmed the theological and missional integrity of the Methodist movement, but insisted they must not separate from the church. Because of this, some of his lay preachers abandoned the movement. They broke ranks and led a minor schism. With this divisive spirit in the air, in 1758 John Wesley published his "Reasons against Separation" as part of a larger work entitled *Preservative Against Unsettled Notions in Religion*. Charles Wesley reinforced John's reasons with the publication of *Hymns for the Use of the Methodist Preachers*, to which he appended John's "Reasons against Separation."

In the first of three sections, John lays out twelve reasons against separation. Fomenting schism, in the Wesleys' view, contradicts their mission, hinders their witness to God's loving purposes, leads to further divisions, fails to serve God, produces evil fruits, increases prejudice, and disturbs peace. The hymns of Charles against separation hardly minced words:

> Pride, only pride, can cause divorce,
>> can separate 'twixt our souls and thee:
> Pride, only pride, is discord's source,
>> the bane of peace and charity:
> But us it never more shall part,
>> for thou art greater than our heart.[23]

To the advocates of separation, John proclaims:

> If it be said, "But at the Church [substitute UMC] we are fed with chaff, whereas at the meeting [substitute GMC] we have wholesome food:" We answer, 1) The prayers of the Church are not chaff: They are substantial food for any who are alive to God. 2) The Lord's Supper is not chaff, but pure and wholesome for all who receive it with upright hearts. Yea, 3) In almost all the sermons we hear there, we hear many great and important truths. And whoever has a spiritual discernment, may easily separate the chaff from the wheat therein.

In his "Reasons Against Separation," Wesley contends with the spirit and the tactics of schismatics:

If we continue in the church not by chance, or for want of thought, but upon solid and well-weighed reasons, then we should never speak contemptuously of the church, or anything pertaining to it. In some sense, it is the Mother of us all, who have been brought up therein. We ought never to make her blemishes matter of diversion, but rather of solemn sorrow before God. We ought never to talk ludicrously of them; no, not at all, without clear necessity. Rather, we should conceal them, as far as ever we can, without bringing guilt upon our own conscience. And we should use every rational and scriptural means, to bring others to the same temper and behavior. I say, All; for if some of us are thus minded, and others of an opposite spirit and behavior, this will breed a real schism among ourselves. It will of course divide us into two parties; each of which will be liable to perpetual jealousies, suspicions, and animosities against the other. Therefore on this account likewise, it is expedient in the highest degree, that we should be tender of the church to which we belong.

John Wesley's late sermon "On Schism" (1786) also bears directly on a spirit of division in the church. In all these documents that advocate a spirit of unity, Wesley provides no hint of doctrinal indifferentism. His adherence to the essentials of faith remains steadfast. Doctrine does matter. In this sermon, however, Wesley provides strong biblical and theological reasons for preserving the unity of the church in the face of doctrinal disagreements. He describes schism as a grievous evil. "To separate ourselves from a body of living Christians, with whom we were before united, is a grievous breach of the law of love. . . . It is only when our love grows cold, that we can think of separating from our brethren."[24]

Separation (division and schism) mitigates against God's loving purposes. It doesn't reflect the spirit of Christ who is always working for good in the world. It damages our witness to the power of God's reconciling love, compromises the love we should have for each other, and threatens the peace and love of our hearts. Separation hurts everyone. Unity, on the other hand, bears testimony to the triumph of love and the possibility of beloved community. One of the ecumenical officers of our church, Jean Hawxhurst, concurs:

> The United Methodist Church has a powerful opportunity to witness to the world that the love of Jesus Christ is stronger than the disagreements that threaten to divide us. Clearly, we are called to let all our relationships be governed by Christ-like love. Staying together is the only witness that lives up to that high calling. Schism does not live up to that calling.[25]

Study and Discussion Questions
for Part I

1. Read Isaiah 43:18-19. Where do you see God doing a new thing in your life, your church, your community, and in the world? What are you doing to nurture this new life? What is your role in this great work of God?

2. Love and unity seem to go together. Both lofty ideals sound good, but we know they aren't easy. What are the things that stand in the way of love and unity in your world? What have you been doing to cultivate deeper love and more inclusive unity?

3. Read Ephesians 4:1-6. This circulated Pauline letter drives home the point of unity. What do each of these "ones" mean to you: body, spirit, hope, Lord, faith, baptism, God and Father of all? How can you live into this vision?

4. Read Isaiah 11:6-9. The prophet provides a vision of life as God intends it to be. What are those things that help move us closer to this dream? Where are you experiencing "beloved community" today and how might you extend it to others?

Part II

A Renewed Wesleyan Movement of Inclusive Love

5

The Opportunity Before Us

In this image there is neither Greek nor Jew, circumcised nor uncircumcised, barbarian, Scythian, slave nor free, but Christ is all things and in all people. Therefore, as God's choice, holy and loved, put on compassion, kindness, humility, gentleness, and patience. Be tolerant with each other and, if someone has a complaint against anyone, forgive each other. As the Lord forgave you, so also forgive each other. (Colossians 3:11-15)

This book begins with a clarion call to renewal and an affirmation that the church always needs to be reformed. In this section we think more about how to recognize a renewed Wesleyan movement of inclusive love. We explore the areas of our church life that require attention. What are our most pressing needs, and what do we need to do to open our hearts and lives to the restorative influence of the Spirit? We stand at such a critical juncture. The fracturing of our church gives pause and a yearning for hope among those who remain. An amazing opportunity opens before us to think deeply, pray hard, and work for renewal. We don't make renewal happen. That's God's work. But God needs willing partners to tend the flame of the Spirit's work. Do you want to be one of those partners?

The title of Section II sends a signal or two about the direction in the second half of this book. Section II of *Multiplying Methodism* by Jeff Greenway and Mike Lowry focuses on "a renewed Wesleyan movement of faith in the Global Methodist Church." *Multiplying Love* offers an alternative vision to theirs in four chapters. Jeff and Mike place great stress on truth, and they identify the recovery of doctrinal integrity as the primary "challenge" of our age. We emphasize inclusive love. For Methodists, everything revolves around God's love. Faith (truth, that is, knowledge of God) is a means; love of God and neighbor is the end or goal. Like those breaking away to emphasize "truth," we need to rediscover what it means to be a movement. But the question remains, What kind of movement should this be? What are the characteristics of this renewed "Wesleyan" movement of "inclusive love"?

When teaching church history, the motif of renewal is typically used to help students gain insight into how God brings about transformation among God's people. As stated in Section I, we often must change in order to be the same. Examples of this pervade the story of the Christian family and the saga of Israel's people before it. The sixteenth-century reformations illustrate how, in that pregnant moment of change, the reformers developed different strategies they thought were faithful in their efforts to renew the church.

Consider the metaphor of a swimming pool. While living in Florida and having a pool that needed maintenance, it became apparent to me how a pool is an analogy for the renewal of a shared Christian life. In the late medieval world, green algae appeared (again) in the corners of the pool (church). A process was afoot that threatened to make the pool unusable. Many believed the pool was increasingly unfit for God's purposes. Something had to change. This mess had to be cleaned up. The Roman establishment said, "Not to worry. We've seen this before. This too shall pass. Simply continue general maintenance, perhaps give a little more attention to it, and all will be well."

Martin Luther, in Germany, feared the situation was too far gone for simple maintenance. He believed the state of the pool required more direct and dramatic action. His solution to the growing problem was to "shock the pool." When a swimming pool reaches a tipping point—more bad than good—it is shocked with hydrochloric acid in order to stabilize it and remove the algae. So Luther shocked the pool with acid—the Word of God. Only scripture, he believed, had the power to deal with the problem properly.

John Calvin approached the problem of his polluted pool with a different strategy. He drained the pool of all the dirty water and set his people to the task of scrubbing it down. Once the pool itself was properly cleaned, he refilled the pool with clean, fresh water. This was his experiment in Geneva. Those who refused to conform to his agenda were invited to leave the city; refugees from England and Europe who warmed to his ideas flooded into the city.

The radical reformers approached the task of renewal more simplistically. The situation was so bad, the condition of the pool so far beyond repair that, they said. "Forget this pool. We just need to build a new pool. Why waste our time attempting to restore something that is beyond repair?"

How does the Wesleys' approach to renewal figure in this analogy? As one might expect, their approach was synthetic. Continue general maintenance; a good idea. Shock the pool; definitely. Jeff and

Mike decry "moralistic therapeutic Deism" in cultured Christianity today. However, Deism and a gospel of "moral rectitude" typified the Enlightenment Anglicanism of the Wesleys' day. Malaise and "doctrinal drift" within the eighteenth-century Church of England called for direct action and innovation. Drain the pool and replace the bad water? Never. The Wesleys believed they could reclaim the water despite its poor quality. Abandon the pool and build a new one? Absolutely not! They genuinely loved their pool. The pool held too many good memories for them, had shaped their lives, and pointed them in the direction of God's love. It had fulfilled its purpose faithfully in so many ways. To discard it would be the height of irresponsibility.

Even more importantly, the Wesleys supplemented maintenance and shock therapy with innovative practices to refresh the pool. They inserted dynamic, spinning vacuum cleaners (Methodist Societies with their classes and bands), cleaning the water, removing the algae, restoring the pool to its healthier state. That was the intent, at least. They introduced these "catalytic agents" to facilitate change. Their prayer was that this continuing work inside the church would refresh it and help it reclaim its reason for being. Rather than separating, they immersed themselves ever more deeply in the pool for the sake of love.

Jeff and Mike claim that "the challenge before us" is "to return to the essence of the gospel message" (p. 73). What they mean by this is a recovery of the doctrinal foundations of Christian orthodoxy. They mean adherence to our United Methodist doctrinal standards. While ordained United Methodists should seriously and faithfully sustain vows to proclaim and live our doctrinal inheritance, the essence of the gospel message is love, not adherence to doctrine.

Jeff and Mike frame their discussion of this challenge in relation to the very personal and even painful question: "Why would anyone want to bother being Christian today?" (p. 74). The logic of their response flows something like this:

1. "We need to separate the Christian faith from American culture. . . . When the culture begins to infiltrate, change, or obliterate what it means to live as God's people—we cease to be the people God calls us to be" (pp. 74-75).
2. The pervasive culture of "Moralistic Therapeutic Deism"[26] has displaced classical Christianity in the church.
3. In the face of the decline of an identifiable "Christian" difference, and in order to answer the why question about being Christian, we need to reclaim Christian "truth."

They infer that The United Methodist Church has succumbed to this aberrant culture. Given the "theological wilderness of today's Methodism" (p. 82), the UMC can't provide a faithful response to the question about "why anyone should be a Christian." In other words, it has no inherent or substantial evangelistic purpose. Bankrupt in its theology and practice, the situation leaves no alternative but separation or disaffiliation. To return to the pool analogy, they feel they have shocked the pool with no success (cf. Luther), and, therefore, must abandon it (prefer radical reform). Unfortunately, this therapy is not Wesleyan, which is the very thing they claim to be.

Nonetheless, Jeff and Mike justify their perspective by quoting John Wesley: "I am sick of opinions. I am weary to bear them. My soul loathes this frothy food. Give me solid and substantial religion. Give me an humble, gentle lover of God and man."[27] Ironically, Wesley's words direct us to the real challenge of our age, but not the one Jeff and Mike identify. Wesley does not define "solid and substantial religion" as doctrinal purity or even adherence to Christian essentials. He defines true religion not in terms of doctrine but in terms of relationships. True religion is "a humble, gentle lover of God and man." He points to love, not to truth.

Let's embrace doctrinal integrity. Let's fully affirm the essentials of faith. But bad doctrine isn't our challenge. Our challenge is how to proclaim and bear witness to God's overwhelming, unconditional love in our various contexts at a time such as this. For whatever reasons, that message of love isn't getting through to a broken, bleeding, polarizing world. "Doctrinal slippage" isn't our problem. Our apparent inability (particularly in our churches) to love others as Christ has loved us presents our most critical challenge. Or does it signal an exciting opportunity?

Let's view the present situation positively as "opportunity"— therefore the title of this chapter—and not negatively as "challenge." Our hearts and minds are drawn to the opportunity to discover and rediscover how to live into the fullest possible love of God and the fullest possible love of everything else in God. This unrelenting love defined the Wesleys' program of renewal. They faced stiff challenges in their own day but turned them into opportunities. Their "presenting issue" was that so many people of their time did not know they were loved. Their simple strategy was to help people fall in love with the God who loved them, and then spread that love lavishly to everyone else. The primary way in which they helped people know they were loved was by loving them. Their strategy was that simple; their plan was that clear.

Nearly three hundred years down the road, God presents us

Methodists with the same opportunity. Our primary questions should be: Do our siblings in the human family know they are loved? In this world, which seems at times oblivious to love, how can we become a solution and not a cause of this disconnect with love? This last question cuts to the chase! Despite the fact that Christians in general and United Methodists in particular think they are loving, those outside the church don't typically perceive this in them, in us.

First, let's look at American conceptions of God. In 2006 the Baylor University Institute for Studies of Religion conducted one of the most extensive religious surveys ever undertaken in the United States—the Baylor Religion Survey. In the first round of its findings entitled "American Piety in the 21st Century," analysts discerned four different conceptions of God among the thousands who participated. Here are their findings and the percentages in each category:

Type A: *Authoritarian God* (31.4 percent). In this view, God engages the world primarily in judgment, meting out punishment for unfaithfulness and ungodliness.

Type B: *Benevolent God* (23 percent). These people view God mainly as a force of positive influence in the world who is primarily good and merciful.

Type C: *Critical God* (16 percent). Among these participants, God views the world critically and unfavorably, rectifying wrongs in this world in another life.

Type D: *Distant God* (24.4 percent). In this view, God
is a cosmic force (a clock maker) who, after
setting the laws of nature in motion, retreats
to a distant, inactive space.

The remaining 5.2 percent, while describing themselves as atheists, may have concerns about
the morality of human behavior and ideals of
social order.[28]

Apparently, only one in four Americans conceives God as benevolent—we might simply say loving. Three out of four, on the other
hand, view God as either authoritarian, critical, or distant, or do not
believe in God at all. They haven't encountered (or have forgotten)
the love of God revealed in Jesus. The most pressing challenge, rather
opportunity, today is to introduce them to a God of love, whose love
for them knows no bounds.

Secondly, let's look at non-Christians' views of Christians. Here
we turn to two different studies. The research team at LifeWay conducted a survey in 2007 and drew the following conclusion: "A
majority of unchurched Americans (79 percent) think that Christianity today is more about organized religion than about loving God
and loving people; 86 percent believe they can have a good relationship with God without being involved in church." Scott McConnell,
associate director of the study, observes:

> Outsiders are making a clear comment that churches are not
> getting through on the two greatest commandments to love
> God and love your neighbor. They see the church as candles,
> pews, and flowers, rather than people living out their love for
> God by loving others. Such skepticism can only be overcome by

churches and believers who demonstrate the unity and love for which Jesus prayed.[29]

A more recent study conducted by Ipsos for The Episcopal Church in the United States, entitled "Jesus in America," suggests that nonbelievers think Christians are hypocritical, judgmental, self-righteous, and arrogant. Christians, in stark contrast, think of themselves as compassionate and loving. By means of this study, the Presiding Bishop of The Episcopal Church, Michael Curry, was hoping to get answers to the question, How are we perceived? He concluded:

> This is a wake-up call for us, and based on what we have learned, we are refocusing our efforts on being a church that looks and acts like Jesus and models its behavior on his teachings. In this process, we hope to ignite a revival of love that encourages all Americans to do a better job of loving their neighbours.[30]

The challenge before us for evangelism and ethics is not doubling down on doctrinal fidelity, as important as doctrine is. Rather we need to embrace the opportunity before us for a revival of love. We need to learn again how to love because God first loved us. We need to become catalysts of love in our church and in our world. We need a renewed Wesleyan movement of inclusive love that breaks down all barriers and affirms that Christ is all and in all. As United Methodists, we need to clothe ourselves with compassion, kindness, humility, meekness, and patience. We need to bear with each other, forgive each other, let the peace of Christ rule in our hearts, and clothe ourselves with love.

In the chapters that follow we envision how radical inclusive love might shape The United Methodist Church as we live into a future filled with hope.

6

The Church as a Community of Inclusive Love and Grace

Remain in me, and I will remain in you. A branch can't produce fruit by itself but must remain in the vine. Likewise, you can't produce fruit unless you remain in me. I am the vine; you are the branches. If you remain in me and I in you, then you will produce much fruit. Without me, you can't do anything.... My Father is glorified when you produce much fruit and in this way prove that you are my disciples. As the Father loved me, I too have loved you. Remain in my love. If you keep my commandments, you will remain in my love, just as I kept my Father's commandments and remain in his love. (John 15:4-5, 8-10)

John Wesley longed for every Methodist to embody what he called genuine Christianity. He urged Methodist communities to love like Jesus loved. He knew that Christian authenticity was crucial to renewal in the church. It also fueled God's mission of love in the world. We know all too well the kind of damage done by those who claim to follow Jesus but bear no resemblance to him. It sounds judgmental to discern the presenting problem, but some forms of Christianity in the United States seem to look nothing like Jesus today. They seem to embrace values antithetical to Jesus's personal witness and teaching, particularly about the reign of God. To put it bluntly, Christians are not always loving.

Christian hypocrisy, as we observed in the previous chapter, turns so many away from the way of Jesus. In his own time, Wesley aimed to avoid this kind of problem. He didn't want anything to stand in the way of people experiencing God's love for them. Tragically, Christians themselves are often the biggest obstacle to God for other people. Thus in 1753 he published a little tract entitled "A Plain Account of Genuine Christianity." He wanted to leave no doubt about his vision of the authentic Christian life. Here, in part, is what he had to say:

> Remembering that God is love, genuine Christians are conformed to the same likeness. They are full of love for their neighbors, of universal love, not confined to one sect or party, not restrained to those who agree with them in opinions or in outward modes of worship or to those who are allied to them by blood or recommended by nearness of place. Neither do they love those only that love them or that are endeared to them by intimacy of acquaintance. But their love resembles that of God whose mercy is over all God's works. It soars above all these scanty bounds, embracing neighbors and strangers, friends and enemies, yes, not only the good and gentle but also the disobedient, the evil and unthankful. For they love every soul that God has made, every child of humanity.[31]

John Wesley devoted his entire life, in fact, to the recovery of this very thing. Here we have a portrait of what an authentic Christian looks like for those who have no idea. This is how an authentic disciple of Jesus lives, filled with love and motivated by mercy and grace. Everything begins with God's love. Everything. Ideally, the church embodies this love as well. It lives in this unbounded love and offers this inclusive love to everyone. Nothing exceeds the dimensions of this love.

Charles Wesley's lyrical paraphrase of Ephesians 3:16-19 celebrates the primary source of their vision:

> O love divine, how sweet thou art!
> When shall I find my willing heart
> all taken up by thee!
> I thirst, and faint, and die to prove,
> the greatness of redeeming love,
> the love of Christ to me.
>
> Stronger his love than death or hell;
> its riches are unsearchable;
> The first-born sons of light
> desire in vain its depth to see.
> They cannot reach the mystery,
> the length, and breadth, and height.[32]

In their chapter on "reclaiming the heart of the Christian faith," Jeff and Mike continue a lament about the post-Christian character of contemporary society. They suggest that the Global Methodist Church will fulfill its calling to be an "in the world but not of it" counter-cultural movement. The foundational framework of their renewed Wesleyan movement consists of four essential pillars. This new church intends to be:

I. *Genuinely orthodox*. The church must "relearn and re-commit" to the "historic theological core of the Christian faith" (p. 85).

II. *Truly Wesleyan.* "Key Wesleyan distinctives," they observe, "will be taught, embraced, and lived out in practice" (p. 86). These include:

1. A high Christology with Jesus as Lord, fully human and fully divine.
2. Sin as a malignant disease.
3. The fullness of salvation in prevenient, justifying, and sanctifying grace.
4. The lived implementation of sanctification.
5. Life as a disciplined follower of Jesus Christ (86-87).

III. *Unashamedly evangelistic.* Offering Christ to others will become a core practice of the Christian faith again.

IV. *Passionately missional.* "A renewed Methodism," Jeff and Mike write, "will be unafraid to confront issues of peace, economic injustice, racism, sexism, and the environment" (p. 91).

Their identification of these four pillars begs the question as to why anyone would need to leave The United Methodist Church to implement their vision? The practices they commend are alive and well today or are critical issues on the radar of those engaged in renewal. Committed United Methodists would simply offer the following response to each of their pillars.

1) The United Methodist doctrinal standards have not and cannot be changed. They articulate a robust understanding of the "received faith tradition" understood as the teaching and witness of the apostolic community. In The United Methodist Church, by and large, the Word is read and preached, and the Sacraments duly administered.

2) The *United Methodist Book of Discipline* articulates the

"Distinctive Wesleyan Emphases" (with many similarities to those re-presented for the GMC) under the rubrics of prevenient grace, justification and assurance, sanctification and perfection, faith and good works, mission and service, and nurture and mission in the church (¶ 102).

3) Evangelism presents many challenges in the church today. Let's reflect on this missional practice of the church more fully here than on the other pillars that Jeff and Mike identify. They claim that "evangelism is about 'tactics for sharing the good news'" (p. 88). Another meaning for the Greek word (*euangelion*) that is rendered as evangelism is "gospel-bearing," and this meaning represents something much larger, more complex, and more exciting than conversion tactics. In the theological instruction that candidates for the ministry receive, they encounter a more robust understanding of evangelism.

At least six principles drawn from the legacy of holistic evangelism in the Methodist tradition provide a platform to rediscover this important practice:

- Evangelism is a vital part of the larger mission of God; it is the essence—the heart—of all Christian mission.
- Evangelism is a process, not simply an effort to secure conversions that are stereotypically experienced in crisis moments in the lives of individuals.
- Evangelism is concerned with making disciples, not simply facilitating conversion; it involves participation in God's process of growing authentic disciples of Jesus.
- Evangelism is oriented toward the reign of God and initiating persons into an alternative community of God's people who give themselves for the life of the world.
- Evangelism is a missional practice of the whole people

69

of God, a set of habituated practices related to being in community; all God's children are "gospel bearers."

- Evangelism is inescapably contextual, involving the Christian community in a complex dynamic interaction of gospel sharing and cultural engagement.[33]

Most conversions during the Wesleyan revival occurred not through preaching or self-initiated conversations with strangers but in the intimacy and fellowship of small groups of people seeking the assurance of God's love.

4) Love is the mission. In the past quarter century, United Methodists made great strides in the recovery of a robust missional vision of the church. In an era when "attractional tactics" are ineffective, more and more churches are discovering hands-on mission as their reason for being.

Continuing Renewal in The United Methodist Church

Renewal in the Wesleyan way revolves around the idea of the church as a community of love and grace. A renewed Wesleyan movement of inclusive love will reflect the four dimensions of love described in a circulating letter to the Ephesians:

1. the height of sovereign grace—the Message,
2. the depth of caring relationship—the Community,
3. the length of Christian pilgrimage—the Discipline, and
4. the breadth of compassionate witness—the Servanthood.[34]

These four inherently Wesleyan ingredients already provide the chemistry for continuing and dynamic Wesleyan renewal in the UMC—a movement in which love and grace saturate our identity.

Message. A recovery of the church as a community of inclusive love and grace begins with the central message (*kerygma*) of the Bible—the proclamation of the death and resurrection of Jesus Christ. This message forms the church. Because of Jesus, we have a wonderful message to proclaim about God's unconditional love and grace for all people in all places and all times. The Wesleys rediscovered this message in their own time. In the midst of polarization and estrangement, we desperately need to sustain this core message of grace and love, proclaiming it through words and lives.

Peter embedded this message in his preaching recorded in the opening chapters of Acts. He proclaimed the dawn of God's inbreaking reign through the self-revelation of God in Jesus Christ and the creation of a new community of grace and love in the Spirit. Likewise, Paul bore witness to the spiritual liberation mediated through self-giving love (cross) and new life in Christ (resurrection). The Wesleys proclaimed the free grace of God and consistently preached about God's inclusive love. Adherence to orthodoxy (or the law) does not constitute the church; the experience of God's grace and love does. This starts with God's message that Paul says should "live in you richly" (Colossians 3:16).

Community. Early Christianity flourished because of the nature of its community (*koinonia*). Connection with God and each other was more than a concept in the early church. It was the primary characteristic of the way the followers of Jesus lived day by day. They "devoted themselves to the apostles' teaching, to the community, to their shared meals, and to their prayers" (Acts 2:42). Gathering around the eucharistic meal as one family in Christ defined who they were.

The earliest Christians and the early Methodists experienced this community as a gracious fellowship with Christ. Connectedness in a partnership of love was one of the hallmarks of early Methodism. Christianity, according to the Wesleys, isn't so much a religion as it is a relationship with God extended into relationships with others. Shared life together was one of the greatest gifts they had to offer to people who were seeking intimacy and love in life. Methodists lived their lives in partnership with each other and in mutually accountable relationships of love. Those within our reach yearn for this kind of community in our church, offered as a gift to others.

Discipline. As a rabbi, Jesus used many different methods to communicate his message of grace and his mission of love to those around him. He was concerned about the process by which his followers might be formed into loving children of God. He knew that most of us are shaped by actions more than anything else. So he introduced his followers to a way of discipline (*paideia*)—practices that form, inform, and transform us spiritually.

Discipline liberates. Unless a student engages in disciplined practice to learn how to play the piano, the learner will never be "free" to release the music from within their whole being. The Wesleys stressed holistic spiritual formation in the Christian life. They believed that faithful discipleship entailed growth of both heart and mind. They nourished the early Methodist people through both Word and Sacrament, personal and social engagement. All this implies a journey—a lifelong process of learning and growth. It entails all those things done in community that shape the whole person in the quest for maturity in Christlike love. Flourishing United Methodist congregations claim this more excellent way in the journey toward the fullest possible love of God and neighbor.

Servanthood. Jesus served others. He taught about the importance and centrality of humility and servanthood (*diakonia*). "Instead, the greatest among you must become like a person of lower status and the leader like a servant," he explained. "So which one is greater, the one who is seated at the table or the one who serves at the table? Isn't it the one who is seated at the table? But I am among you as one who serves" (Luke 22:26-27). He left no doubt that he was the chief of servants (see John 13). The hallmark of Jesus's life was the way he cared for the needs of people around him. He demonstrated compassionate love toward everyone.

Every practice and habit in the Wesleyan portrait of the Christian life points to servanthood as modeled by Jesus and rooted in love. The breadth of compassionate witness is the fruit of discipleship, expressed through mission and service in the life of the church. Charles Wesley advocated an incarnational ministry and identified service as the primary call of the church in every age:

> A charge to keep I have,
>   a God to glorify,
> a never-dying soul to save,
>   and fit it for the sky.
> To serve the present age,
>   my calling to fulfill;
> O, may it all my powers engage
>   to do my Master's will![35]

These four ingredients reveal the Wesleys' vision of the church and its gracious mission of love in the world. It begins with the message of God's good news in Jesus Christ, the story of his death and resurrection. Your experience of love and grace in Christ immediately draws you into a community where you learn how to love. In the context of this new family, you receive the discipline and engage in those practices necessary for you to be nourished and grow in your faith. All Christians find their ultimate purpose in servanthood. Just as in Jesus's image of the vine and the branches (John 15), we are gathered to learn how to love (as disciples) and then sent out into the world (as apostles) to share that love with others.

This experience of the gospel—not our doctrine related to it—provides the foundational framework of a renewed Wesleyan movement of love and grace. This love is the heart of the Christian faith, and for Christ's sake, let's shock our churches with more excellent love.

7

Discovering Love Again
for the First Time

We love because God first loved us. Those who say, "I love God"
and hate their brothers or sisters are liars. After all, those who
don't love their brothers or sisters whom they have seen can hardly
love God whom they have not seen! This commandment we have
from him: Those who claim to love God ought to love their brother
and sister also. (1 John 4:19-21)

While writing this book in my room at Sarum College in Salisbury, England, I rejoiced to hear the bells of the magnifi-
cent cathedral just outside my window. This is a magical place. To
"change ring," as it is called, you need a "peal of bells." *Peal* is the
term used for a set of bells, but it can also refer to the sound they
make. The word *peal* comes from "appeal" actually, which is what
bells are designed to do. They appeal, or we could say make their
appeal, to those who hear them. This English practice of "change
ringing" is an analogy to something important about love.

A peal of bells is rung by a band of bell ringers. In change ringing, bells are rung in a sequence. They don't play a tune or melody. Moreover, they are rung in a different order in each sequence. Some changes are simple; others are extremely complex. To ring the changes requires discipline, practice, and teamwork. The variations are endless. The combinations boggle the mind. Are you ready for this? In a peal of ten bells, known as a royal, there are 3,628,800 possible sequences. You ring all these different possibilities to create beauty and to elevate the spirit. To love as Christ has loved us requires discipline, practice, and teamwork. The possibilities of love are endless. You can't exhaust love.

This analogy about the bells pertains to the discussion of the previous chapter and provides a segue into this one. The bells proclaim a *message* of beauty and goodness. It takes a *community* to create the sound. *Discipline* plays a central role in even making the ringing of the bells possible. The ringers are *servants* dedicated to something larger than themselves. The bells peal out, as it were: community, variety, purpose—love. Because change ringing never repeats exactly the same pattern, one bell ringer told me "It is like discovering love again for the first time." This chapter explores the endless possibilities of love.

Chapter 7 in Jeff and Mike's book looks at "a renewed Methodism in the life of the local church." It provides a template, as it were, including some key elements and some faithful practices, for the renewal of the Wesleyan tradition as they envisage it. They distinguish their vision from what they call a "culturally mainline dying older version of Wesleyan witness" (p. 97). Their seven key elements can be clustered into three distinct emphases or key words.

First, *diverse*. Their renewed Methodism, as they aspire, will be diverse. It will represent a new ethnic and cultural mix. It will be composed of a working and middle-class constituency. It will elevate the importance of indigenous leadership with regard to theological and spiritual formation. Second, *orthodox*. They return to their primary themes of high Christology, biblical authority, and a commitment to historic Christian orthodoxy. Third, *transformed*. This new church will emphasize transformation—defined as "real conversion" in and through Jesus Christ—and the power and presence of the Holy Spirit.

Four "faithful practices" will also define their aspirations for a separatist Methodism. First, the church will be "mission driven." Second, reflecting their rejection of a "big tent philosophy," it will potentially restrict itself to a "discipled membership." In other words, all members of the Global Methodist Church will be expected to engage in "faith sharing and hands-on ministry." Third, small group discipleship will figure prominently in the program of Christian practice. Fourth, worship will be "a counter-cultural activity" (p. 100).

In response to this aspiration for a renewed yet separated Methodism, consider an alternative Wesleyan vision. The vision of United Methodism (always reforming) is rooted in the key elements of the Wesleyan revival, which was generated from John and Charles's rediscovery of boundless, inclusive love. Some of these elements, naturally because they were formed in United Methodist institutions, would be endorsed as Jeff and Mike's aspiration for a breakaway organization. But to make the critical distinction, there is no appeal here to orthodoxy or even doctrine. Neither do most Methodists pit the Christian faith against a culture-gone-wrong. Rather, the United Methodist way of life rests on the perennial need of the church to discover love again for the first time.

In a sermon entitled "On a Single Eye," published within a year of his death, John Wesley proclaimed: "How great a thing it is to be a Christian, to be a real, inward, scriptural Christian! Conformed in heart and life to the will of God!"[36] Wesley's primary concern—what our primary concern should be—is the realization of God's rule in the life of every person and in our world. His language about God's will and God's rule all point to love. Love is his singular focus. He reaches forward toward Christian wholeness, for holiness of heart and life, meaning the fullest possible love of God and all else in God. Renewal means the rediscovery of inclusive love.

This is the kind of renewal we long to see in The United Methodist Church. We have the opportunity beyond schism to embrace six movements of the Spirit. These movements open doors to the wondrous world of inclusive, expansive, unbounded love.

I. Living Word

The Wesleys rediscovered the Bible for their own time. We need to rediscover the Bible today. They concluded quite early in life that scripture bore witness, more than anything else, to the love and grace of God in Christ for all people. They believed that whenever individuals or communities engage the words of scripture and invite the Holy Spirit into that dynamic conversation, the "dead" words become the "living Word" for us.

Preaching the Word became John's primary medium for celebrating God's love and sharing it with others. Here is how he described the purpose of his preaching:

> What religion do I preach? The religion of love—the law of kindness brought to light by the gospel. What is this good for? To make all who receive it enjoy God and themselves, to make

them, like God, lovers of all, contented in their lives and crying out at their death in calm assurance, "O grave, where is thy victory? . . . Thanks be unto God, who giveth *me* the victory, through *my* Lord Jesus Christ."[37]

In his hymns, Charles describes the love he discovers in the written Word. God's love is ceaseless and unexhausted, unmerited and free, faithful and constant, unalterably sure. The God of the Bible delights, helps, waits, saves. Moreover, the full energy of God's love and grace extends to every creature, "enough for all, enough for each, enough for evermore."[38] The Wesley brothers poured all their energies into the proclamation of this good news of God's love revealed in the living Word. We aim to reclaim this legacy in our own time.

II. *Saving Faith*

The Wesleys discovered that whenever the Word came to life for those they sought to serve, the experience of faith came hot on its heels. Charles and John both define the gift of faith as the capacity to trust God. Living faith as absolute trust in God through Christ, nurtured in fellowship, is the Methodist staff of life. Like many Christians, even today, the Wesley brothers believed they first had to make themselves acceptable to God. But they ultimately came to realize that God had loved them all along. Like a spiritual sunrise, it dawned on them that God's presence and love had accompanied them each step of their journey. The unconditional love of God in Christ freed them and opened to them a whole new world of joy, peace, and inner healing. They called this "saving faith."

Having encountered God's unconditional love in the Jesus of the Gospels, those touched and transformed by God's grace become the instruments of that same love in the world. The experience of God's love leads to faith, and faith leads to the desire to share love with others. Faith is a means to love's end. Faith works by love (Galatians 5:6). The phrase "faith working by love leading to holiness of heart and life" expresses the essence of the gospel proclamation of free grace. Saving faith not only revives the fainting heart, it also breathes new life into the heart of the church. We need this today.

III. *Holistic Spirituality*

One of the means to spiritual vitality in the Wesleyan movement of renewal was the dynamic interrelation of "works of piety" and "works of mercy." Works of piety are simply what we mean by classic spiritual disciplines. They include prayer, immersion in scripture, Christian fellowship, and participation in the sacrament of Holy Communion. Works of mercy consist essentially of serving God and one's neighbor in the world. Broadly they include acts of compassion (personal practices) and acts of justice (social practices). Piety and mercy, when held together, reshape or conform our lives to the image of Christ. By immersing ourselves in these disciplines, we seek to be truly Christlike in our attitudes, actions, and words. Devoid of compassion, works of piety can become pharisaical. Works of mercy, when not rooted in a grace-filled relationship with God, can become bankrupt and fatigued. But when held together, they enable love to flourish in our lives.

John Wesley describes the importance of both kinds of practice:

> As the love of God naturally leads to works of piety, so the
> love of our neighbour naturally leads all that feel it to works of
> mercy. It inclines us to feed the hungry; to clothe the naked; to
> visit them that are sick or in prison; to be as eyes to the blind
> and feet to the lame; an husband to the widow, a father to the

fatherless. . . . it is an infallible truth that
> All worldly joys are less
> than that one joy of doing kindnesses.[39]

The Wesleys affirmed that no act of worship or devotion related to the love of God was complete until we carry God's love into the world in concrete acts of compassion and justice. To engage in these disciplines renews the soul and re-energizes the church. Each generation needs to rediscover this rich and holistic form of Christian spirituality.

IV. *Accountable Discipleship*

Whenever teaching about early Methodism, the whole movement (and method) can be summarized in two words: accountable discipleship. John Wesley defines a Methodist as someone who has universal love filling the heart and governing the life. But this love-filled life doesn't just happen. A Methodist is a person who wants to experience love and to love as Jesus loved, more than anything else in life. In this regard, James K. A. Smith reminds us about the most important question Jesus asks of each of us:

> "What do you want?" That's the question. It is the first, last, and most fundamental question of Christian discipleship. In the Gospel of John, it is the first question Jesus poses to those who would follow him. . . . Jesus doesn't encounter you and me and ask, "What do you know?" He doesn't ask, "What do you believe?" He asks, "What do you want?" This is the most incisive, piercing question Jesus can ask us precisely because we are what we want.[40]

The Wesleys knew that the Spirit must teach us how to love if that is what we truly want. We apprentice ourselves to the master of

Multiplying Love

love. By means of this accountable lifestyle we cultivate holy habits—works of piety and works of mercy—in which we practice love. The Wesleys encouraged their followers to watch over each other in love. Accountable discipleship means to help each other along the way toward deeper love of God and neighbor—holiness of heart and life. Growth in grace and love are only possible, the Wesleys believed, when we live out our faith in intimate communities of love. Renewal in The United Methodist Church can hardly be aspired without a return to a form of accountable discipleship that facilitates ongoing growth in love.[41] We yearn to recover this kind of spiritual intimacy today.

V. *Formative Worship*

The Wesleyan movement of renewal was both an "evangelical" and a "eucharistic" revival. Worship forms the people of God. Our engagement in adoration, repentance, forgiveness, thanksgiving, proclamation, and praise in a worshipping community teaches us how to love. Both spoken words and enacted signs shape us into a people of love. Little wonder that our worship consists of preaching and the sign-act of Holy Communion. It was impossible for the Wesleys to think about the spoken word (preaching) apart from the word made visible (eucharist). Let's celebrate how Word and Table shapes United Methodists now and will continue to do so into our future.

In United Methodist worship, sacred song renews us in a holistic way. It engages the whole of who we are. "The eighteenth-century revival," Richard Heitzenrater observes, "was to a great extent borne on the wings of Charles's poetry. Charles's hymns not only helped form the texture of the Methodist mind but also, perhaps more importantly, set the temper of the Methodist spirit."[42] For my purposes here it suffices to acknowledge that the hymns of Charles Wesley functioned as catalysts of renewal and rebirth in the lives of the Methodist people. Music, in new and varied forms, continues to do this in us and for us. Hymns and spiritual songs are a powerful tool in the Spirit's work of renewal. We need to sing together and celebrate the goodness of God more often and more joyfully.

VI. *Missional Vocation*

The Church of England in the Wesleys' day was an institution in need of repair. It had exchanged its true mission (to love and serve) for maintenance and position, and many among us sense a similar problem after fifty years of United Methodist polity. The church can become distant from and irrelevant to the world it is called to serve during a time of tremendous change. Its forms and its structures can become inflexible and devoid of life (particularly during demographic and economic decline) so that the weight of its "institutionalism" is quenching the Spirit and suffocating the life of God's people. It needs the reviving breath of a new spirit. It needs to rediscover its identity as God's agent of love in the world.

The Wesleys' understanding of the church was essentially formed around mission. Charles expressed it so potently in a well-known couplet: "To serve the present age, / My calling to fulfill." All their energy was directed toward the empowerment of Christ's faithful disciples in ministry to God's world. Indeed, they all viewed evangelism and mission—the proclamation of God's love in word and deed, in witness and service—as the reason for their existence. They learned how to love through discipleship and worship and were then sent out to share that love with others, singing their faith along the way. The

Wesleyan Way is one of incarnational ministry that empties itself of all but love and finds its greatest reward in the realization of God's dream of shalom for all.

A Vision for the Refreshed United Methodist Church

I know the plans I have in mind for you, declares the LORD; they are plans for peace, not disaster, to give you a future filled with hope. When you call me and come and pray to me, I will listen to you. When you search for me, yes, search for me with all your heart, you will find me. (Jeremiah 29:11-13)

When we came home from mission service in Zimbabwe, we made our home in Westerville, Ohio. As I surveyed our new property, I found a spindly, decayed plant in our back yard. After a little investigation, I discovered that it was a grape vine. Neglected, abandoned, and untended, it had simply grown wild, and more importantly, unproductive. It had no grapes. Not being a vinedresser, I basically chopped away at the eyesore until it looked a little more respectable and forgot about it. A long time later, low and behold, it started producing grapes again. It needed to be refreshed.

The United Methodist Church needs to be refreshed. Jeff and Mike feel that its state is so moribund (this would be the right word) that it is beyond recovery. So they have left it. I affirm that our beloved church needs renewal. In some areas of the church's life we need radical reform, but most of us are far from abandoning it. Rather, we choose to remember who we are. We choose to rediscover the practices that create healthy, vital Christians and communities. We aim to commit ourselves anew to love. We open our hearts to the love that God longs to pour into us. We share that love extravagantly, lavishly to all around us who don't know that God loves them desperately. We open our arms to all and embrace the gifts of all, and all means all. Together and united we cultivate a vision for the ever-refreshing United Methodist Church and trust that God will give us a future with hope.

Jeff and Mike, in their chapter about "a vision for the Global Methodist Church" envisage a church of "like-minded, warm-hearted, Jesus-loving, Spirit-filled, Wesleyan, orthodox Christians" (pp. 107-108). We anticipate no problems with a warm-hearted, Jesus-loving, Spirit-filled vision. Each of us should aspire to those qualities. "Like-minded," however, is a troubling requirement. In the face of inevitable differences in theology and practice, not to mention fickle human nature within any group, John Wesley embraced diversity so long as it did not break the bond of love. Love was more important to him than doctrinal uniformity.

We are also concerned about the terms *orthodox* and *Wesleyan*, because of the way these words are used—that is, what they mean. And here Jeff and Mike appear to be right about some deep differences in language among Methodists. I consider myself to be an "orthodox Christian," but I oppose doctrinal uniformity if it preempts love. For me, while I consider both words to be important, love always takes precedence over doctrine. In the ecumenical movement during the twentieth century, a distinction was made between "Faith and Order" and "Life and Work." Both are important, but in the final analysis, most Methodists have always leaned in the direction of the latter. What we do is more important than what we say we believe. While we affirm the doctrinal standards of our tradition, we can be dubious about how well Methodists, lay and clergy, really understand them or have migrated with other meanings from a different Christian tradition.

Several themes in our heritage stand out. A Wesleyan vision begins with a platform of grace. While concerned about the law, its primary concern is the law of love. Wesleyan Christians assume a posture of humility in relation to others. Our history demonstrates the importance we have placed on the practice of inclusivity. We have had to repent (change our hearts and minds) many times over the years for our blindness to the inclusion of "others." When we have been at our best, however, (meaning Christlike) we have been radically inclusive. We have sought to measure all we are and do against the promise of love.

In light of these language differences and others, Jeff and Mike offer ten reasons for joining the Global Methodist Church. At this point in time, these remain aspirational, but they are obviously significant and portray the ethos of this new, severed community:

1. Consistent Faithfulness in Doctrine
2. Reclaim Accountable Discipleship
3. Church Planting
4. Mission Driven Rather than Structurally Bound

5. Term-limited Episcopacy
6. Systemic Accountability
7. Lean Bureaucracy—Lower Costs—No Trust Clause
8. More Congregational Input on Clergy Selection
9. Easier Path to Ordination
10. Global from Day One

Some of these reasons we might agree with on face value as an expression of our Wesleyan heritage at its best, as discussed earlier in this book. This is certainly true with regard to reclaiming accountable discipleship (United Methodist Discipleship Ministries has extremely helpful resources in this arena), engaging in church planting (UMFX, United Methodist Fresh Expressions is pioneering such work), and re-energizing a missional vision of the church ("missional church" literature in United Methodism abounds). Why would anyone not aspire to be global given the communication technologies that collapse distance across our world? A hearty yes to that as well. The issue of "consistent faithfulness to doctrine" depends on who is interpreting the sources for its definition.

Most eye-opening in this list of reasons are the five (half) pertaining to church polity. What's the motive of those abandoning an "institutional" form of church for another in which half the stress is placed on organizational and administrative concerns? It's hard to understand how term-limited episcopacy, for example, would be a deal-breaker for anyone.

Their position to revoke the "trust clause" completely pulls this new church beyond the parameters of historic and standard Wesleyan thought and practice. Clearly, a creeping "congregationalism" pervades several of these reasons and displaces Methodist "connectionalism" in this new church. One wonders how American culture (an influence so frequently vilified in Jeff and Mike's book) figures in this dramatic shift? As a lifelong theological educator on three continents, I have a few ideas about how to revise the (expensive) way we prepare servants for ordained ministry. But how does an "easier path" to ordination serve the churches well? The ethos that undergirds these "political" concerns simply seems to reflect a different view of church than that envisioned by the Wesleys.

I co-chaired a World Methodist Council/Baptist World Alliance Dialogue, and the ten reasons to join the Global Methodist Church "feel" like a document our Baptist colleagues might have drafted. I don't mean that pejoratively, in any way. I love my Baptist brothers and sisters, but The United Methodist Church offers a different vision of Christian faith and practice.

What concerns us most about Jeff and Mike's vision is the way in which it diverges sharply from a genuinely Wesleyan vision. The portrait of the Global Methodist Church they paint is congregational in polity (not connectional), creedal in orientation (not oriented around "practical theology" in the service of "faith working by love"), and essentially exclusivist (not inclusive in vision, despite its "global" title).

I feel compelled to stay in The United Methodist Church. The reign of God is much larger than any one church or denomination. We must always remember this. But we also need to plant ourselves in some part of God's vineyard. Here are five reasons, then, to stay in or join—even celebrate—all that God has done and is doing in The United Methodist Church. These five reasons also serve as a paradigm of renewal for a refreshed church. An excerpt is provided from either the writings of John or Charles Wesley to underscore each point.

1) *Wide Embrace*. The United Methodist Church has a wide, gracious, and loving embrace. The church most people yearn for is a community of faith that puts love at the very center of its life and mission. This openness to all people, including people different from me or you, as unique siblings deeply loved by God characterizes The United Methodist Church we know. All God's children are invited to put their gifts to use in the service of God's reign of reconciliation.

John Wesley describes Methodists in this way in his sermon on "Catholic Spirit:"

> They love one another as friends, as companions in the Lord, as members of Christ and children of God, as joint partakers now of the present kingdom of God, and fellow heirs of God's eternal Kingdom. All of whatever opinion or worship or congregation who believe in the Lord Jesus Christ, who love God and neighbor, who rejoice to please and fear to offend God, are careful to abstain from evil and zealous of good works. Those disciples are of a truly catholic spirit who bear all these continually upon their hearts, who, having an unspeakable tenderness for their persons and longing for their welfare, do not cease to commend them to God in prayer, as well as to plead their cause before others. They speak comfortingly to them and labor by all their words to strengthen their hands in God. They assist them to the uttermost of their power in all things, spiritual and temporal. They are ready "to spend and be spent for them," even to lay down their lives for their sake.[43]

2) *Christlike Practice*. The United Methodist Church aspires to be Christlike in practice. As we observed, numerous surveys over the past decades demonstrate that the majority of people in the United States view the church as judgmental. Jesus gives us a different model

of relating to the world and others. The United Methodist Church seeks to cultivate disciples of Jesus who are like him—merciful, compassionate, and forgiving.

Perhaps no hymn better expresses the character of the disciple whose mind is conformed to that of Christ than Charles's lyrical reflection on the Beatitudes.

> Come, thou holy God and true!
>   Come, and my whole heart renew;
> Take me now, possess me whole,
>   form the Savior in my soul.
>
> Happy soul, whose active love
>   emulates the blest above.
> In thy every action seen,
>   sparkling from the soul within.[44]

3) *Scriptural Dynamism.* The United Methodist Church is shaped by a dynamic view of scripture. It is strongly biblical in its orientation. The Bible is the bedrock upon which the faith of United Methodist identity is built. But its view of the Bible is not simplistic; rather, like Wesley, it embraces a dynamic conception of scripture as the "living Word." Antithetical to literalistic and legalistic views of scripture, the United Methodist view offers a rich, robust, indeed a scriptural foundation for life in the triune God.

John Wesley bears testimony to the centrality and importance of scripture in his life:

> Let me be *homo unius libri*. Here then I am, far from the busy ways of life. I sit down alone. Only God is here. In God's presence I open, I read the book for this end, to find the way to heaven. Is there a doubt concerning the meaning of what I

read? Does anything appear dark or intricate? I lift up my heart to the Father of Lights. . . . . I then search after and consider parallel passages of scripture, "comparing spiritual things with spiritual." I meditate thereon with all the attention and earnestness of which my mind is capable.[45]

4) *Spiritual Growth.* The United Methodist Church is deeply concerned about growth in grace. Not so much invested in believing the right things, its primary passion is translating God's love into action in life. It elevates the importance of practices of piety, such as prayer, but also advocates acts of mercy—compassion and justice for all. The United Methodist Church offers a holistic spirituality that refuses to separate the spiritual from the concrete realities of life.

In his *Plain Account of the People Called Methodists,* John Wesley defended the accountable discipleship that characterized the Methodist movement of renewal. We need opportunities to grow in every age of the church.

> Who marked their growth in grace? Who advised and exhorted them from time to time? Who prayed with them and for them as they had need? This, and this alone, is Christian fellowship. But, alas! Where is it to be found? Look east or west, north, or south; name what parish you please. Is this Christian fellowship there? Rather, are not the bulk of the parishioners a mere rope of sand? What Christian connection is there between them? What intercourse in spiritual things? What watching over each other's souls? What bearing of one another's burdens? . . . We introduce Christian fellowship where it was utterly destroyed. And the fruits of it have been peace, joy, love, and zeal for every good word and work.[46]

5. *Missional Character.* The United Methodist Church is missional in character. It lives not for itself but for others. It is missional

in its design to partner with God in God's great work of love in the world. Its fundamental orientation is outward, spun out in the life of the world to wage peace, work for justice, and emulate the "beloved community" God desires for all.

Charles Wesley sings about mission as the joyful offer of boundless love:

> I would the precious time redeem,
>   and longer live for this alone.
> To spend and to be spent for them
>   who have not yet my Savior known.
> Fully on these my mission prove,
>   and only breathe to breathe thy love.
>
> Enlarge, enflame, and fill my heart
>   with boundless charity divine.
> So shall I all my strength exert,
>   and love them with a zeal like thine.
> And lead them to thine open side,
>   the sheep, for whom their shepherd died.[47]

I love The United Methodist Church, but I don't "worship" it. We put it in danger if we ignore some of the critical issues requiring our attention. For too many years we have relied on a Christendom model of membership and have failed to cultivate generations of faithful disciples of Jesus. We still struggle with the eroding effects of racism that mitigate against our movement toward God's vision of the human family. Apart from some exceptional (aging) programs in the church, such as *Disciple*, we haven't helped postmodern Christians engage scripture in a way that brings it to life. Perhaps most significantly, we haven't engaged the changing cultures in which we are immersed in anything approaching a healthy dialogue. We have no other place to live in Christ than in our own neighborhoods. We must understand them more fully and embrace them with the love of Christ.

Inclusive love, in fact nothing more and nothing less, must be the foundation of a renewed Methodism. Wesley made this abundantly clear in his day and we need to do everything possible to demonstrate Christlike love in our church and in our world today. John Wesley provides the template:

> Let love not visit you as a transient guest, but be the constant ruling disposition of your soul. See that your heart is filled at all times and on all occasions with real, genuine benevolence, not to those only that love you, but to every soul. Let it pant in your heart, let it sparkle in your eyes, let it shine on all your actions. Whenever you open your lips, let it be with love, and let the law of kindness be on your tongue. Your word will then distill as the rain and as the dew upon the tender herb. Be not constrained or limited in your affection, but let it embrace every child of God.[48]

Let's pray that the Spirit of Christ will refresh us all and help us multiply love in The United Methodist Church for the sake of the world.

Study and Discussion Questions for Part II

1. In a circulating letter that reached the Colossians (3:11-15), Paul talks about clothing ourselves with love. "Put on compassion, kindness, humility, gentleness, and patience. Be tolerant with each other and, if someone has a complaint against anyone, forgive each other." Many people see Christians today as judgmental and hypocritical. How do we "change into clothes" that communicate we are an inclusive and loving community?

2. Read John 15:4-5, 8. What do you think Jesus means by "remaining" in the vine? What practices help us remain in Christ? And what about the fruit? What fruit do you and your church family produce that help others taste and see that God is good?

3. Chapter 7 identifies five movements of the Spirit that help us discover love again for the first time. Which "practices" do you feel drawn to most naturally? How have you expe-

rienced these in your own life? Which does your church emphasize?

4. Read Jeremiah 29:11-13. All day long God is working for good in the world. Where do you see God at work for good in your own life and the life of your church? What seed of hope is God planting right now? What is your greatest hope for the church and the world?

Epilogue

Our world needs a multiplication of love. As Methodists we need to experience God's multiplication of love in our individual lives. The people and leaders of The United Methodist Church need to reaffirm our calling to be a connected community in which love multiplies.

When the Wesleys experienced the unconditional love of God in Christ and developed a clear vision of their purpose in life as God's beloved children, they made the pursuit of holiness of heart and life their singular goal. To them this meant the fullest possible love of God and the fullest possible love of all else in God. J. Ernest Rattenbury once wrote that Charles Wesley's life "might be summed up compendiously in one phrase: 'a quest for love.' "[49]

For each of us and among all of us, this quest means a spiritual journey into Christlikeness. As apprentices of Christ, we work with the Spirit to expand God's love in our hearts and lives. When people see us, then they see Christ. We come to resemble Jesus, both as individuals and as church. Whenever others read our lives and our life together in the beloved community, as certainly they will, the word *love* would be the first word that comes to mind.

Light attracts. Light chases away the darkness. We are drawn to the light, and if we permit it to fill our lives, it shines through us. The light of love dispels every form of darkness. The shining lives of God's redeemed and restored children have a critical role to play in the unfolding of God's reign. Each of us has a place in this great work, and our beloved church has a place in this as well. Those who radiate the love of God draw others into the reign of God.

We pray for the inbreaking of the glorious light of the One "whose glory fills the skies." I pray that you will make the prayer and vision of Charles Wesley your own so that we might multiply God's love in The United Methodist Church and throughout our world together:

> Come, our holy God and true!
> Come, and my whole heart renew.
> Take me now, possess me whole.
> Form the Savior in my soul.

> Happy soul, whose active love
> emulates the blessed above.
> In my every action seen,
> sparkling from the soul within.

> We to every sufferer nigh,
> hear with deep concern the cry
> of the widow in distress,
> of the poor and fatherless!

The weak hands, we lift them up,
bid the helpless mourners hope.
Give to those in darkness light,
guide the weary wanderer right.

Through the influence of your love,
tenderness, compassion, move:
love immense and unconfined,
love to all of humankind.

Love, which wills that all should live.
Love, which all to all would give.
Love, that over all prevails.
Love, that never, never fails.[50]

Endnotes

1. Dag Hammarskjöld, *Markings*, Leif Sjöberg & W. H. Auden, trans. (New York: Alfred A. Knopf, 1965), 89.
2. Daily Morning Prayer: Rite Two, *The Book of Common Prayer*, bcponline.org/DailyOffice/mp2.html.
3. John and Charles Wesley, *Hymns and Sacred Poems* (London: Strahan, 1739), 169.
4. Magrey deVega, "Clergy Session, Opening Remarks, Thursday, June 8, 2023," 3-4 (personal copy).
5. Prior biblical and theological works include: (affirming) Steve Harper, *Holy Love: A Biblical Theology of Human Sexuality* and Mike Regele, *Scripture, Science and Same-Sex Love*, or (opposing) Robert Gagnon, *The Bible and Homosexual Practice*. These three Abingdon Press books include bibliographies.
6. For in-depth treatment, see Steve Harper, *Holy Love: A Biblical Theology of Human Sexuality*.
7. John Wesley, *The Works of John Wesley, Volume 7, A Collection of Hymns for the Use of the People Called Methodists*, ed. Franz Hildebrandt and Oliver A. Beckerlegge (Oxford: Clarendon Press, 1983), 194-95.
8. John Wesley, *The Works of John Wesley, Volume 1, Sermons I, 1-33*, ed. Albert C. Outler (Nashville: Abingdon Press, 1984), 67.

9. Paul W. Chilcote, "'Practical Christology' in John and Charles Wesley," in *Methodist Christology: From the Wesleys to the Twenty-First Century*, ed. Jason E. Vickers and Jerome Van Kuiken (Nashville: Wesley's Foundery Books, 2020), 5.

10. See Steve Harper, *Five Marks of a Methodist* (Nashville: Abingdon, paperback 2022) for an interpretation of "The Character of a Methodist."

11. Sometimes Wesley used the term opinions somewhat indiscriminately and synonymously with doctrine, so one must be careful in applying this distinction. See Randy L. Maddox, "Opinion, Religion, and 'Catholic Spirit': John Wesley on Theological Integrity," *Asbury Theological Journal* 47, 1 (1992): 63–87.

12. John Wesley, *The Works of John Wesley, Volume 9, The Methodist Societies: History, Nature, and Design*, ed. Rupert E. Davies (Nashville: Abingdon Press, 1989), 227.

13. One of his most extensive accounts of essentials appears in Wesley's Letter to a Roman Catholic (sections 6-10), in which he seeks to demonstrate the broad range of doctrinal consensus between them. See Albert C. Outler, ed., *John Wesley* (New York: Oxford University Press, 1964), 494-96.

14. Wesley, *Works*, 9:254-55.

15. John Wesley, *The Works of John Wesley, Volume 2, Sermons II, 34-70*, ed. Albert C. Outler (Nashville: Abingdon Press, 1985), 374. In this quotation, Wesley uses "opinion" in the sense of "doctrine." So read "doctrine" here.

16. Paul W. Chilcote, "Theological engagement and doctrinal standards," Section 1.2.2, in "Methodist Theology," *St. Andrew's University Encyclopaedia of Theology*; https://www.saet.ac.uk/Christianity/MethodistTheology.

17. John and Charles Wesley, *Hymns on the Lord's Supper* (Bristol: Farley, 1745), 7.

18. "An Order for Morning Praise and Prayer," *The United Methodist*

Hymnal (Nashville: The United Methodist Publishing House, 1989), 877.

19. See Kenneth L. Smith & Ira G. Zepp, Jr., *Search for the Beloved Community: The Thinking of Martin Luther King, Jr.* (Valley Forge: Judson Press, 1974), 119-40.

20. Walter Brueggemann, *Living Toward a Vision: Biblical Reflections on Shalom* (Cleveland: United Church Press, 1976), 20.

21. Charles Wesley, *Hymns for the Nativity of Our Lord* (London: Strahan, 1745), 23-24.

22. Ironically, they do not see the message of Acts 15 as a primary justification for the full inclusion of the queer community in the life of the church. They even quote the text: "Why then are you now challenging God by placing a burden on the shoulder of those disciples [Gentiles] that neither we nor our ancestors could bear?" Simply replace Gentiles—the outside group, despised by the Jews— with queer siblings.

23. Charles Wesley, *Hymns for the Methodist Preachers* (London: Strahan, 1760), 14.

24. John Wesley, *The Works of John Wesley, Volume 3, Sermons III, 71-114*, ed. Albert C. Outler (Nashville: Abingdon Press, 1986), 64.

25. Heather Hahn, "What John Wesley teaches about church unity," *UM News*, December 7, 2016; https://www.umnews.org/en/news/what-john-wesley-teaches-about-church-unity.

26. Moralistic therapeutic deism is a syndrome defined in a study of religious beliefs in 2005 among USA teenagers by Notre Dame sociologist Christian Smith. The phrase was then filtered through Reformed evangelical perspectives in a Barna study.

27. John Wesley, *The Works of John Wesley, Volume 11, The Appeals to Men of Reason and Religion*, ed. Gerald R Cragg (Oxford: Clarendon Press, 1975), 321. If they were to have cited the full quotation, they would have seen that it adds even greater weight to the centrality of love. Wesley says, "Let my soul be with these Christians [i.e., those

who practice love], wheresoever they are, and whatsoever opinion they are of."

28. *American Piety in the 21st Century: New Insights to the Depth and Complexity of Religion in the US: Selected Findings from The Baylor Religion Survey*, September 2006; https://www.baylorisr.org/wp-content/uploads/2019/09/American-Piety-Finall.pdf.

29. Audrey Barrick, "How Do Unchurched Americans View Christianity?" *The Christian Post*, January 9, 2008; https://www.christianpost.com/news/how-do-unchurched-americans-view-christianity.html.

30. Rebecca Paveley, "American Christians seen as 'hypocritical' and 'judgmental', study suggests," *The Church Times*, March 18, 2022; https://www.churchtimes.co.uk/articles/2022/18-march/news/world/american-christians-seen-as-hypocritical-and-judgemental-study-suggests.

31. Outler, *John Wesley*, 184.

32. Charles Wesley, *Hymns and Sacred Poems*, 2 vols. (Bristol: Farley, 1749), 1:58.

33. Paul W. Chilcote and Laceye C. Warner, eds., *The Study of Evangelism: Exploring a Missional Practice of the Church* (Grand Rapids: Eerdmans, 2008), xxvi-xxvii.

34. I have drawn this template of Christian renewal in the Wesleyan way from my book, *Recapturing the Wesleys' Vision: An Introduction to the Faith of John and Charles Wesley* (Downers Grove, IL: InterVarsity Press, 2004).

35. Charles Wesley, "A Charge to Keep I Have," *The United Methodist Hymnal*, 413.

36. John Wesley, *The Works of John Wesley, Volume 4, Sermons IV, 115-151*, ed. Albert C. Outler (Nashville: Abingdon Press, 1987), 121.

37. Wesley, *Works*, 11:51.

38. Charles Wesley, *Short Hymns on Select Passages of the Holy Scriptures*, 2 vols. (Bristol: Farley, 1762), 1:53-54.

39. Wesley, *Works*, 3:191.

40. James K. A. Smith, *You Are What You Love: The Spiritual Power of Habit* (Grand Rapids: Brazos Press, 2016), 1-2.

41. See the sermon "On Zeal," John Wesley's template for a form of Christian discipleship that cultivates love; Wesley, *Works*, 3:308-21.

42. Quoted in S T Kimbrough, *Lost in Wonder* (Nashville: The Upper Room, 1987), 11-12.

43. Wesley, *Works*, 2:94-95.

44. Wesley, *Hymns and Sacred Poems* (1749), 2:138-39.

45. Wesley, *Works*, 1:104-106.

46. Wesley, *Works*, 9:259.

47. Wesley, *Hymns and Sacred Poems* (1749), 1:301.

48. Wesley, *Works*, 3:422-23.

49. J. Ernest Rattenbury, *The Evangelical Doctrines of Charles Wesley's Hymns* (London: Epworth Press, 1941), 278.

50. Wesley, *Hymns and Sacred Poems* (1749), 2:138-39; modernized and modified.

Sources

American Piety in the 21st Century: New Insights to the Depth and Complexity of Religion in the US: Selected Findings from The Baylor Religion Survey, September 2006; https://www. baylorisr.org/wp-content/uploads/2019/09/American-Piety-Finall.pdf.

Barrick, Audrey. "How Do Unchurched Americans View Christianity?" *The Christian Post,* January 9, 2008; https:// www.christianpost.com/news/how-do-unchurched-americans-view-christianity.html.

Brueggemann, Walter. *Living Toward a Vision: Biblical Reflections on Shalom.* Cleveland: United Church Press, 1976.

Chilcote, Paul W. "Methodist Theology." *In St. Andrew's University Encyclopaedia of Theology*; https://www.saet.ac.uk/Christianity/MethodistTheology.

Chilcote, Paul W. *Recapturing the Wesleys' Vision: An Introduction to the Faith of John and Charles Wesley.* Downers Grove, IL: InterVarsity Press, 2004.

Chilcote, Paul W. and Laceye C. Warner, eds. *The Study of Evangelism:*

Exploring a Missional Practice of the Church. Grand Rapids: Eerdmans, 2008.

deVega, Magrey. "Clergy Session, Opening Remarks." Florida Annual Conference, The United Methodist Church, Lakeland, Florida, Thursday, June 8, 2023.

Hahn, Heather. "What John Wesley teaches about church unity." *UM News*. December 7, 2016; https://www.umnews.org/en/news/what-john-wesley-teaches-about-church-unity.

Kimbrough, Jr., S T. *Lost in Wonder*. Nashville: The Upper Room, 1987.

Maddox, Randy L. "Opinion, Religion, and 'Catholic Spirit': John Wesley on Theological Integrity." *Asbury Theological Journal* 47, 1 (1992): 63–87.

Outler, Albert C., ed. *John Wesley*. New York: Oxford University Press, 1964.

Paveley, Rebecca. "American Christians seen as 'hypocritical' and 'judgemental', study suggests." *The Church Times*, March 18, 2022; https://www.churchtimes.co.uk/articles/2022/18-march/news/world/american-christians-seen-as-hypocritical-and-judgemental-study-suggests.

Rattenbury, J. Ernest. *The Evangelical Doctrines of Charles Wesley's Hymns*. London: Epworth Press, 1941.

Smith, James K. A. *You Are What You Love: The Spiritual Power of Habit*. Grand Rapids: Brazos Press, 2016.

Smith, Kenneth L., and Ira G. Zepp, Jr. *Search for the Beloved Community: The Thinking of Martin Luther King, Jr.* Valley Forge: Judson Press, 1974.

Vickers, Jason E. and Jerome Van Kuiken, eds. *Methodist Christology: From the Wesleys to the Twenty-First Century*. Nashville: Wesley's Foundery Books, 2020.

Wesley, Charles. *Hymns and Sacred Poems.* 2 vols. Bristol: Farley, 1749.

Wesley, Charles. *Hymns for the Methodist Preachers.* London: Strahan, 1760.

Wesley, Charles. *Hymns for the Nativity of Our Lord.* London: Strahan, 1745.

Wesley, Charles. *Short Hymns on Select Passages of the Holy Scriptures.* 2 vols. Bristol: Farley, 1762.

Wesley, John. *The Works of John Wesley. Volume 1. Sermons I, 1-33.* Edited by Albert C. Outler. Nashville: Abingdon Press, 1984.

Wesley, John. *The Works of John Wesley. Volume 2. Sermons II, 34-70.* Edited by Albert C. Outler. Nashville: Abingdon Press, 1985.

Wesley, John. *The Works of John Wesley. Volume 3. Sermons III, 71-114.* Edited by Albert C. Outler. Nashville: Abingdon Press, 1986.

Wesley, John. *The Works of John Wesley. Volume 4. Sermons IV, 115-151.* Edited by Albert C. Outler. Nashville: Abingdon Press, 1987.

Wesley, John. *The Works of John Wesley. Volume 7. A Collection of Hymns for the Use of the People Called Methodists.* Edited by Franz Hildebrandt and Oliver A. Beckerlegge. Oxford: Clarendon Press, 1983.

Wesley, John. *The Works of John Wesley. Volume 9. The Methodist Societies: History, Nature, and Design.* Edited by Rupert E. Davies. Nashville: Abingdon Press, 1989.

Wesley, John. *The Works of John Wesley. Volume 11. The Appeals to Men of Reason and Religion.* Edited by Gerald R. Cragg. Oxford: Clarendon Press, 1975.

Wesley, John and Charles. *Hymns and Sacred Poems.* London: Strahan, 1739.

Wesley, John and Charles. *Hymns on the Lord's Supper.* Bristol: Farley, 1745.